MASTER-PLANNED COMMUNITIES

LESSONS FROM THE DEVELOPMENTS OF CHUCK COBB

Early Forms of Smart Growth

KALVIN PLATT

Urban Land Institute

ABOUT THE URBAN LAND INSTITUTE

The Urban Land Institute is a nonprofit research and education organization whose mission is to provide leadership in the responsible use of land and in creating and sustaining thriving communities worldwide.

The Institute maintains a membership representing a broad spectrum of interests and sponsors a wide variety of educational programs and forums to encourage an open exchange of ideas and sharing of experience. ULI initiates research that anticipates emerging land use trends and issues and provides advisory services, and publishes a wide variety of materials to disseminate information on land use development.

Established in 1936, the Institute today has nearly 30,000 members and associates from some 92 countries, representing the entire spectrum of the land use and development disciplines. Professionals represented include developers, builders, property owners, investors, architects, public officials, planners, real estate brokers, appraisers, attorneys, engineers, financiers, academics, students, and librarians.

ULI relies heavily on the experience of its members. It is through member involvement and information resources that ULI has been able to set standards of excellence in development practice. The Institute is recognized internationally as one of America's most respected and widely quoted sources of objective information on urban planning, growth, and development.

Copyright 2011 by the Urban Land Institute

Printed in the United States of America. All rights reserved. No part of this book may be reproduced in any form or by any means, electronic or mechanical, including photocopying and recording, or by any information storage and retrieval system, without written permission of the publisher.

Library of Congress Cataloging-in-Publication Data

Platt, Kalvin.
 Master-planned communities : lessons from the developments of Chuck Cobb / Kalvin Platt.
    p. cm.
 ISBN 978-0-87420-161-1
 1. Planned communities--United States. 2. Cobb, Chuck. I. Title.
 HT169.57.U6P59 2011
 307.76'80973--dc23
                              2011020259

ULI Catalog Number: M89

All photographs are by Tom Fox unless otherwise noted.

AUTHOR

Kalvin Platt
Consulting Principal
The SWA Group
Sausalito, California

PROJECT STAFF

Gayle Berens
Senior Vice President
Education and Advisory Group

Adrienne Schmitz
Senior Director, Publications

Theodore Thoerig
Manager, Awards and Publications

James Mulligan
Managing Editor

Laura Glassman
Publications Professionals LLC
Manuscript Editor

Betsy VanBuskirk
Creative Director

John Hall
John Hall Design Group
Book and Cover Designer
www.johnhalldesign.com

Craig Chapman
Senior Director, Publishing Operations

REVIEWERS

Todd Mansfield
Principal
Mansfield Company LLC
Charlotte, North Carolina

H. Pike Oliver
Senior Lecturer
Cornell University Program in Real Estate
Ithaca, New York

Robert Sharpe
Managing Partner
Rancho Sahuarita
Tucson, Arizona

Don Whyte
President
Kennecott Land
South Jordan, Utah

About the Author

For several decades, Kalvin Platt was the lead planning consultant to Charles Cobb at the Arvida Corporation and other development organizations. Platt oversaw design and planning for the firm's master-planned communities at Boca Raton, Longboat Key, Weston, Sawgrass, and Cocoplum in Florida and Willow Springs in Georgia. He then oversaw master plans at Walt Disney World and the University of Miami. Joining the firm of Sasaki, Walker and Associates in 1967, Platt participated in planning work for Cobb at Rancho California.

For 34 years, Platt was president, CEO, and then chairman of Sasaki, Walker and Associates and its successor firm, the SWA Group, an international landscape design and planning firm. He continues as a member of the board of directors and as a consulting principal. His more than 50 years of experience as a planner and urban designer include creating the first comprehensive plan for Metropolitan Miami-Dade County, Florida; acting as planning consultant to several cities for their general plans; and creating a downtown zoning plan for San Francisco, a plan for Griffith Park in Los Angeles, and the plan for the 100,000-acre Golden Gate National Recreation Area for the National Park Service.

In addition to his work with Cobb, Platt's experience in master-planned communities includes the University Park Community, the 30,000-acre Central Irvine Ranch Plan, and the 1,700-acre Village of Woodbridge—winner of a 1994 ULI Award for Excellence, all for the Irvine Company, and the Mountain House New Town and Tejon Ranch Vision Plan, also in California. Some of his other master-planning work includes the Elkhorn and Sun Valley master plans in Idaho, the Alphaville Lagoa dos Ingleses new town in Brazil, coastal plans for the cities of Long Beach and San Diego, and several master-planned communities in China, Japan, and the Philippines.

Platt is a Fellow of the American Institute of Architects, and he holds a degree in architecture from the University of Florida and a graduate degree in city planning from Harvard University. He taught the development studio at Harvard University Graduate School of Design from 1980 to 1982 and was a founding member of the Sustainable Development Council and vice chairman of the Recreation Council at the Urban Land Institute. He coauthored the "Sustainable Land Planning" chapter of the 2005 ULI book *Green Office Buildings: A Practical Guide to Development* and the *Urban Land* magazine articles "City Greenways" and "Lessons from Boca Raton."

WILLIAM TACHAM

Acknowledgments

I want to thank my close collaborators on this work, Charles Lockwood, author and columnist, for his sage advice and editing, always spurring me on, and Tom Fox, whose photographs make the book come alive. Also Chuck Cobb and the six participants in the "Cobb Web" interviews—John Temple, Frank Zohn, Scott Morrison, Gary Derck, Gary Engle, and Peter Rummell—shared their time, knowledge, and experiences in making these communities happen. Many thanks also go to Todd Mansfield, Pike Oliver, Bob Sharpe, and Don Whyte for their cogent review of the manuscript on behalf of the Urban Land Institute.

The depth of experience and sound advice of Adrienne Schmitz, senior director of ULI publications, really made a huge difference in bringing this book together. Gayle Berens, senior vice president at ULI, saw the potential of this work as a ULI publication. John Hall of John Hall Design produced an exciting graphic design and Laura Glassman of Publications Professionals LLC edited the text. Also making essential contributions at critical times were Leah Thompson and Matt Myers at SWA Group, Ambassador Sue Cobb and Mary Jo Klotz at Cobb Partners, Jola Shraub at Durango, and Sandy McKay at Kirkwood. Dorothy Swearingen of NC Mountain Life contributed her beautiful fall color photographs of Cullasaja in the North Carolina Smoky Mountains. Thanks to Kathy Irwin for her photos of Willow Springs. Finally, many thanks go to the residents, employees, and managers of the communities that were studied and visited for this book. Their kind cooperation, hospitality, and evident enthusiasm for their communities were the truest reflection of the value of all our efforts.

Patience is a necessary virtue for the family of a book author. Janne and I made it to 50 years married during this book's writing and publication, and she showed very clearly the patience and forbearance that made both possible. She, with my son, David, and daughter, Andrea, offered support and a sounding board that helped me through this intense, sometimes painful, but in the end rewarding year looking back over 40 years.

Kalvin Platt

Contents

PREFACE | VII

1 | A FIRSTHAND LOOK AT MASTER-PLANNED COMMUNITIES AND SMART GROWTH | 2

Controlling Suburban Sprawl | 6
Evaluating Master-Planned Communities and Smart Growth | 8
Defining the Future of Smart Growth in the Suburbs | 11
Characterizing the Master-Planned Communities of Chuck Cobb | 13

2 | COBB'S MASTER-PLANNED COMMUNITIES | 14

Starting in 1967, Chuck Cobb was CEO or chairman of a succession of companies that developed master-planned communities. This chapter presents the communities he developed as CEO or chairman of the respective development firm.

Rancho California, Temecula and Riverside County, California | 16
McCormick Ranch, Scottsdale, Arizona | 28
Arvida at Boca Raton, Boca Raton and Palm Beach County, Florida | 38
Longboat Key Club, Town of Longboat Key, Sarasota County, Florida | 56
Weston, Broward County, Florida | 66
Sawgrass, St. Johns County, Florida | 78
Willow Springs, Roswell, Georgia | 88
Cocoplum, Coral Gables, Florida | 92
Coto de Caza, Orange County, California | 100
The Walt Disney World Resort, Lake Buena Vista, Florida | 106
Cullasaja Country Club, Highlands, North Carolina | 118
Fisher Island, Miami Beach, Florida | 120
Kirkwood Mountain Resort, Kirkwood, California | 126
Durango Mountain Resort, La Plata and San Juan Counties, Colorado | 130

3 | COBB'S ROLE CHANGES | 136

The master-planned projects that follow were developed when Cobb was not the CEO but a member of the board of the development entity.

Telluride Ski and Golf Resort, Telluride, Colorado | 138
Tubac Golf Resort and Spa, Tubac, Arizona | 142
Carillon Park, Tampa Bay, Florida | 146
WCI Master-Planned Communities, Bonita Springs, Florida | 150
University of Miami Campus, Coral Gables, Florida | 154

4 | LESSONS LEARNED: COBB'S MASTER-PLANNED COMMUNITIES AND SMART GROWTH | 160

Strategic Public and Private Planning | 165
Protect Local Heritage—and Profitability | 169
Master-Planned Communities as Economic Engines | 174
Creating Physical and Social Community | 176
Providing Education and Health | 180
Protecting Open Space, Natural Landscape, and Agricultural Resources | 182
Housing Affordability | 184
Transportation and Land Use | 187
A Better Way for Greenfield Development | 192
Conclusion | 193

BIOGRAPHY OF CHARLES E. COBB | 194

Camelback greenway at McCormick Ranch.

Preface

This book draws from my experience of more than 50 years as a planner and designer of master-planned communities throughout the United States and internationally. Two events led me to write this book. The first was a conversation about the success of master-planned communities with Charles "Chuck" Cobb, my client of over 30 years and one of the most creative community developers in the nation. We particularly discussed the many communities with which we had personal involvement. We wanted to answer one question: Did they create economically and environmentally sound communities and a livable quality of life overall? To use a present-day term: Did they pioneer "smart growth"?

The second event that led to this book was my memory of reading a 2002 article on this subject in the *Journal of the American Planning Association* by Ann Forsyth, a professor at the University of Minnesota. I then read—and told Chuck about—her subsequent 2005 book, *Reforming Suburbia: The Planned Communities of Irvine, Columbia, and The Woodlands*, that elaborated on the *JAPA* article. Forsyth documents how these planned communities of the 1960s and 1970s were precursors to what is now termed "smart growth."

From these events came the idea to write a book about Chuck Cobb's master-planned communities, all known for a distinctive and consistent high quality. My firm and I planned many of these communities, which were developed in the fast-growing suburbs of metropolitan America, mostly in the booming Sunbelt states of Florida, California, and Arizona. They vary widely in size, scope, amount of open space, and mix of uses. Some are large, full-service communities, whereas others are infill developments or constitute significant portions of established cities or towns. Some focus on major recreational amenities and function as resorts with retirement or second homes and a strong lifestyle orientation. One is a university campus. All but one of the developments in this book were successfully built out as planned, with some modifications over time to adapt to changing lifestyles and market conditions. Nearly all were economically successful enterprises.

Chuck Cobb's long career in real estate development started in 1964 and continues today. Beginning with Kaiser Aetna, where he led the development of the 95,000-acre Rancho California planned community, and going on to the Arvida Corporation, where he created and led the organization that planned and developed 30 master-planned communities in Florida, Georgia, California, and North Carolina, to the Disney Company where he led Disney Development Company, which helped transform the Disney attractions into full-fledged destination resorts, and on to Cobb Partners where he continues today with the four-season Kirkwood and Durango Mountain resorts in California and Colorado. This book begins with 15 of Cobb's most significant communities (14 case studies, plus one sidebar) initiated during his time as chairman or CEO of the development company and then highlights other development activity with Cobb's involvement not as CEO, but as a member of the board of the developing entity. In each of these cases, he was able to use the master planning and development skills he honed as CEO to help shape these communities.

The extensive use of current photographs in the book portrays the kind of communities these have become through a careful process of planning and controlled development. The final chapter summarizes the lessons learned from the firsthand experiences in planning and developing these diverse master-planned communities. We hope these lessons will be valuable for today's planners, developers, and elected officials. In particular, we want the evolving principles of smart growth to benefit from our early attempts to make growth "smart." We hope that smart growth continues evolving to meet changing conditions of market, financial mechanisms, transportation, energy, and building technologies to remain the basis of best practices for suburban growth and development.

BELOW
Cocoplum, in Coral Gables, Florida.

We must acknowledge the many talented people of the "Cobb Web" (see page 5), who were recruited, encouraged, and empowered to plan, develop, and bring the communities into existence. These best and brightest executives, managers, and consultants brought their individual energy and creativity to Cobb's overall vision of the highest-quality development and services. They all contributed in making them true communities, unique to their locale and successful over time for their residents and businesses. As a convention, we use the shorthand "Cobb communities" throughout the book, but we do so in full recognition of the team effort involved in this kind of complex enterprise, which took many years and many people to successfully accomplish.

MASTER-PLANNED COMMUNITIES

LESSONS FROM THE DEVELOPMENTS OF CHUCK COBB

Early Forms of Smart Growth

RIGHT The Walt Disney World Resort, Florida; BELOW Old Town Temecula, part of Rancho California.

A Firsthand Look

at Master-Planned Communities and Smart Growth

THE ANTECEDENTS OF SMART GROWTH

go back to carefully planned late-19th-century communities like Riverside and Lake Forest, Illinois, and the early 20th-century Garden City movement based on the writings of Sir Ebenezer Howard in his 1902 book, *Garden Cities of Tomorrow*. In the United States, these, and green-belt communities such as Radburn, New Jersey, influenced development practices in the well-planned streetcar suburbs of the 1920s and 1930s, but in most places such planning was not reinforced by public policy.

With the advent of the interstate highway system, post–World War II growth was characterized by a chaotic patchwork of single-use development: residential subdivisions, shopping malls, and office and industrial parks surging outward from existing cities and suburbs. These scattered developments lacked amenities, open space, and civic facilities and threw infrastructure costs, traffic, and visual unsightliness on adjacent cities and towns. The rapid suburban growth and sprawl that emerged from the dominance of the automobile and the interstate highway network created pressure for more effective and workable ways to guide and control growth.

During the 1960s, an academic interest in the European New Town Movement and the public's rising environmental awareness prompted a number of attempts at controlling growth in various places throughout the United States. These efforts were largely confined to grassroots movements in locales such as Portland, Oregon, and Palo Alto and Petaluma, California.

Learning from garden cities and greenbelt communities, visionary developers in the 1960s and 1970s began to reshape growth by creating the master-planned communities of Reston, Virginia; Columbia, Maryland; The Woodlands, Texas; and Irvine, Valencia, and Westlake in southern California.

Also under planning and development during this era were several of the Cobb master-planned communities covered in this book, including Rancho California, McCormick Ranch, and the early Arvida communities. This time, instead of just being well-executed singular examples, these high-profile communities inspired many master-planned developments throughout the country. Also at this time, substantial public policy at the federal level—most environmentally based—supported these developments with the National Environmental Policy Act in 1969, the Clean Air and Clean Water acts, and endangered species legislation. Many state acts followed that required special studies of environmental impact and set up elaborate systems for controlling growth. The high energy of environmental protection groups pushed much of this policy toward limiting or even stopping growth, even if it was part of a comprehensively planned community.

Not until the 1990s did the state of Maryland shift from just *controlling* growth to *planning* for growth in a landmark, comprehensive, statewide smart growth law that used incentives and disincentives to preserve farmlands and open space and to concentrate development in areas

BELOW Weston Park of Commerce, west of Fort Lauderdale, Florida; **OPPOSITE** Entrance to Durango Mountain Resort, Colorado.

with urban infrastructure. Other states, such as Florida, New Jersey, and Oregon, adopted Maryland's philosophy, and many local governments adopted portions of this new approach to shaping growth.

In response to increasing concerns about the need for a coordinated national approach to managing urban growth, the U.S. Environmental Protection Agency in 1996 formed the Smart Growth Network (www.smartgrowth.org), a nationwide partnership of nonprofit and governmental organizations. Its objective was to create and popularize more formalized growth policies that would boost the economy, protect the environment, and enhance community vitality and residents' quality of life. The Smart Growth Network's partners included environmental groups, historic preservation organizations, professional planning organizations, developers, real estate interests, and state and local governments.

The network has subsequently agreed on 10 Smart Growth Principles to define the basic ingredients of smart growth. They are

1. **MIX LAND USES.**
2. **TAKE ADVANTAGE OF COMPACT BUILDING DESIGN.**
3. **CREATE A RANGE OF HOUSING OPPORTUNITIES AND CHOICES.**
4. **CREATE WALKABLE NEIGHBORHOODS.**
5. **FOSTER DISTINCTIVE, ATTRACTIVE COMMUNITIES** with a strong sense of place.
6. **PRESERVE OPEN SPACE,** farmland, natural beauty, and critical environmental areas.
7. **STRENGTHEN AND DIRECT DEVELOPMENT** toward existing communities.
8. **PROVIDE A VARIETY OF TRANSPORTATION CHOICES.**
9. **MAKE DEVELOPMENT DECISIONS PREDICTABLE,** fair, and cost-effective.
10. **ENCOURAGE COMMUNITY AND STAKEHOLDER PARTICIPATION** in development decisions.

The Cobb Web

"NO ORGANIZATION CHARTS!" was Chuck Cobb's emphatic direction. His management philosophy was a lean, horizontal structure devoid of multi-layered decision making and the stacks of little boxes typical of organization charts. On the basis of his hands-on experience with multiple master-planned communities at Kaiser Aetna, Arvida, and Disney Development, Cobb had set up a decentralized, entrepreneurial system in which executives were treated like partners, each with a high degree of autonomy in his marketplace.

A graduate of Stanford Business School, Cobb built teams of the best and brightest, drawn from prestigious business schools such as Harvard, Wharton, and Stanford, mostly young, and many with some experience in successful ventures. Job responsibilities were woven around the gifts and talents of the individuals, carefully nurtured in Cobb's vision of integrity and quality, and watched over but not dominated by tough financial types, all of whom had bought into the Cobb Web.

The Cobb Web had no rigid boxes where people kept only to their position, and all teammates were expected to step out of their defined roles to help one another maintain the overall level of quality and excellence that Cobb demanded. The companies were designed to give management enough flexibility to successfully respond to the differing market and political conditions throughout the planning and build-out phases of the communities.

John Temple understood the Cobb Web better than anyone. As a fellow Stanford MBA and U.S.

Navy officer, Temple was Cobb's partner at Rancho California and McCormick Ranch in Arizona, and then following Cobb to Florida, he served as president to Cobb's CEO at Arvida and Arvida/Disney. In Temple's words, "The key to success was that the core group stayed small because the business is cyclical ... only four guys working on Rancho California. We wanted the best, we paid for the best, and we were able to keep the best in that way ... two financial whizzes from Stanford ... analyzing how to go about the business.

"In getting the land, we studied the landowners as well as the property. We set up the financial arrangements to make the deal work for the seller—very tax-friendly arrangements. We could use the solid corporate balance sheet to swing the deal, which gave us a competitive advantage. I was the acquisition guy [at Kaiser Aetna]. Chuck took over the development and the operation of the communities.

"At McCormick Ranch we wanted to avoid just being a resort or retirement community. We worked >>>

A 2006 study initiated by the Lincoln Institute of Land Policy, *Evaluating Smart Growth*, examined the effectiveness of smart growth policies since the 1990s in eight states, and it found that no single state did well on all principles, but many succeeded in specific policies that were their high priorities.

In recent years, many supporters of smart growth have discounted master-planned communities as just another form of suburban sprawl. Much of this criticism is because most of these communities were built on greenfields—agricultural or open lands at the edges of cities or in rural areas. Another major criticism is based on the automobile orientation and low densities that were fostered by the interstate highways and suburban lifestyles of the late 20th century. Recognizing today's concerns about energy use, climate change, and greenfield land preservation, a careful look the history of master-planned communities in terms of smart growth principles offers many insights and lessons for today's developers.

CONTROLLING SUBURBAN SPRAWL

More than three decades before the Smart Growth Network was established, Kaiser Aetna Real Estate, under the leadership of group president Chuck Cobb, was building several large-scale planned communities. Because no other company in the United States at that time was taking on multiple master-planned communities, a new business was created that offered a unique opportunity to tap into the public desire for alternatives to sprawl and to earn excellent returns on these investments. Cobb launched this new development model at Kaiser Aetna and later went on to pursue multiple planned developments at the Arvida Corporation, Disney Development, and elsewhere. At Arvida, where he was chief executive officer, Cobb created teams to plan and complete more than 30 master-planned communities in California, Florida, and Georgia. Other large development companies throughout America soon followed suit, taking on the building and marketing of multiple master-planned communities.

The master-planned communities of the 1960s and 1970s were different from the usual suburban sprawl for several reasons. First, they were planned to contain a balanced mix of land uses, including a variety of housing types, employment centers, retail uses, and recreational amenities. They included jobs as well as housing; provided sites for schools, parks, churches, and civic centers; and encouraged cultural, medical, and educational institutions to locate within their boundaries. A real incentive existed to enter as many market segments as possible to smooth out cycles and increase absorption in these large and long-term developments and to offset the large upfront investment in infrastructure and amenities.

Thus, people could live, work, shop, and engage in the myriad of social and civic activities that create community, all within relative proximity. Second, these communities were environmentally sensitive and included ample open space and permanent natural areas. Third, the master-planned communities were large in size, typically ranging from 5,000 to 10,000 acres, but they could be as large as 95,000 acres. They included a full-service infrastructure of roads, utilities, and urban services with mechanisms to finance and maintain these necessary features over time. Finally, they were controlled by a master developer who established guidelines and controls to promote the quality of design and implementation and to create physical unity. The master developer set up community associations to ensure continuity of quality control as the developer relinquished ownership. In almost all cases, these associations continue to the present to maintain landscaping and common areas and facilities and to control new or revised development.

OPPOSITE **Fisher Island, Miami Beach, Florida;** *BELOW* **Arvida Park of Commerce in Boca Raton, Florida.**

Master-planned communities gained popularity, particularly in high-growth regions of the Sunbelt, as people saw the many advantages they offered over unplanned neighborhoods. In the beginning, homes in these communities typically outsold and fetched higher prices than standard suburbia, and they maintained that advantage over time. Because master-planned communities derive much of their desirability from their planning and control of physical attributes, homeowners generally are invested in maintaining these qualities. Businesses were attracted by controlled business environments and good homes for workers. The successes made these privately financed, market-driven master-planned

Arvida Park of Commerce

>>> hard with economic development for jobs and tax base, and we set a standard. The competitors had to meet it and the municipalities started to require it.

"Chuck kept asking me to come to Florida—so many opportunities in Florida. We transferred the California leading-edge expertise to Florida (Bill Shubin from Kaiser to head up commercial and industrial, Roger Hall from Kaiser to head up Boca West and Weston). We brought in Kalvin Platt and other consultants from California. We pursued our whole thesis—have better planning, a sense of place, build a community, higher quality, get a premium ... we were pioneers in Florida doing that. We could charge 10 to 20 percent more. Today those communities have held their values.

"The jurisdictions saw what we had done at Boca West and wanted more of it: we created property tax value, more mixed use, more variety in housing, shops close to residences, town centers. ... We were innovators in protection of natural habitat, golf courses for real golfers—and the expansion of the clubs is phenomenal. We had a better product and a better system: each community had its own management team."

Frank Zohn saw the Cobb Web from his roles as an Arvida corporate executive and then chief financial officer. He offers this perspective: "The single biggest reason for Arvida's success: bright people

worked in an entrepreneurial way in a decentralized structure that gave autonomy within a larger structure. Our people in the various markets knew their consumer. They felt the development was theirs ... a pride of ownership. And they knew it would have been extremely difficult to have played on such a big field—or to have readily raised the capital or gotten the sites outside the Web. Young people could work, grow, and blossom. Cobb created an organization for the entrepreneurs to stay and flourish although they weren't their own boss; we had strong corporate controls. The role of the people in the corporate environment was to make sure it achieved Arvida quality and budget goals.

"Large-scale community development takes time and real estate is cyclical: some good, some not so good. We bought projects that were troubled—possibly because of inadequate capital, overinvestment, bad planning. ... We often got the best locations. We got the site cheap, and it allowed us to do good things: make the necessary changes to make it a success, to catch the upturn. ... We understood the business of community building.

"The master-planned communities have held their quality and value, and have stood the test of time. We didn't build the clubhouses too big for the community to operate. We knew when we left, the community would have to pay for it. >>>

Entrance to
McCormick Ranch
in Scottsdale,
Arizona.

communities profitable for the developer and able to maintain their quality and profitability over many years. For homebuyers, this longevity provided an incentive to maintain the quality, sense of community, and high-than-average property values over the years.

EVALUATING MASTER-PLANNED COMMUNITIES AND SMART GROWTH

Of particular significance, these early communities were financed, developed, and managed as "real world" profit-making enterprises, not one-time-only demonstration projects. The smart growth policies and actions of the public sector set a framework, but the private sector actually builds the communities. Often, these master-planned communities went beyond the smart growth principles to include innovations in marketing and communicating their value to homebuyers, businesses, and the diverse mix of institutions and organizations that make a complete community. They provided assistance to help create good school systems, and they used creative club memberships, sports, recreation centers, and community events to facilitate early onset of the activities that make a vital community. These communities donated or made available at special terms sites for schools; parks; and religious, social, and civic institutions. They offered innovative and diverse residential products, further enriching community life.

Many municipalities, such as Scottsdale, Arizona (see discussion on the McCormick Ranch), recognized that planned communities offered high standards of development, provided infrastructure that the city had difficulty financing, and set up multiple layers of design control and maintenance relieving long-term burdens on the city treasury. In these cases, local governments provided incentives for the growth of master-planned communities to facilitate local growth.

Professor Ann Forsyth studied three iconic master-planned communities of the 1960s and 1970s: Irvine, California; Columbia, Maryland; and The Woodlands, Texas. In her 2002 article in the *Journal of the American Planning Association* and her subsequent well-documented 2005 book,

>>> We wanted something consistent with the lifestyle: the Boca consumer was different from Weston. We set up a structure of community and homeowners associations—you have a mechanism to keep the community fresh, the inner workings that sustain a community."

Scott Morrison saw the Cobb Web from his roles as the operating general manager of the Boca Raton Hotel and Club and head of the hospitality division of Arvida and Arvida/Disney. "Consistent with Cobb's philosophy, we remained thin in our staffing; we outsourced so we could be flexible in a downturn. The [Boca Raton] hotel had to lead the way not only in quality standards for hospitality but also as a key asset in attracting homebuyers for real estate sales. We generated a lot of leads and retained the five-star, five-diamond ratings and image. We were one of two resorts in the United States that had both.

"As an operator you put out a business plan, had the usual tussle with the marketing guy, CFO, and controller, but once you agreed on the plan, you were on your own—you were empowered to get it done. We had wonderful meetings. I never felt so energized as when I came out of meetings with the team. The only time you might get interrupted is if you had to change the plan or explain a negative variance from it.

"Part of the management philosophy was to bring the operator in at the planning and programming stage. I had major input in the program for any community, particularly the clubs. We always set the pace over other clubs and resorts—we wanted the best management we could find. Originally, we gave away the club membership with the purchase of residential property; later on, we charged everyone. The Boca Raton Hotel club turned out to be an enormous profit center for the resort. Some mistakes were made in the few cases in which we were not part of the original planning, and the facilities were underdesigned and required costly remedies. We got that corrected. Finally—and I cannot say it enough—it was a privilege and a joy to work with Chuck and his people."

Gary Derck was a relative newcomer to the Cobb Web, joining Cobb in 1999 as the CEO of Kirkwood Mountain Resort and then moving to take the reins at the Durango Mountain Resort. In his words, "Chuck's core philosophy was to integrate the business models and goals of his development companies with his operating companies, creating a synergistic circle whereby the resort operations attract new real estate prospects, and the new owners benefit the operations and become loyal repeat/referral visitation and business. This approach proved particularly fortuitous in the recent recession where positive cash flow from the operations provided the crucial >>>

Reforming Suburbia, she carefully relates these communities to the principles of smart growth and to recently built new urbanist and smart growth communities. Her conclusions, in brief, follow:

- **THESE COMMUNITIES OF THE 1960S AND 1970S** originated from the concern with the problems created by that era's rapid suburban sprawl and the entrepreneurial opportunities that these problems presented to large, quality-minded developers.

- **THESE COMMUNITIES INTRODUCED** and refined many of the techniques currently promoted by the smart growth movement to combat sprawl, such as a strong sense of place and preservation of environmentally sensitive areas.

- **THESE COMMUNITIES SUCCEEDED** in most of the smart growth principles, but their particular lack of success in providing affordable housing and transportation choices raises the question whether the current smart growth proposals in these areas need to be revised to raise their chances of success.

- **THESE COMMUNITIES MET MOST** of the Smart Growth Network's principles of 1996, except connection to existing communities and collaborative planning, and even these features have been incorporated as the developments aged.

- **THESE MASTER-PLANNED COMMUNITIES** were important generators of high-tech and knowledge-based employment, and they remain so today. National and international technology companies sought out high-quality suburban environments for their facilities and employees' lifestyles.

- **NEW URBANIST APPROACHES** that consider various scales of development—the block, the neighborhood, and the region—closely mirror the issues considered in the master-planned communities. Smart growth strategies such as clustering development to preserve open space, mixing housing types, and creating a sense of identity were all issues new community developers dealt with in previous decades.

- **RESIDENT SURVEYS THROUGHOUT THE DEVELOPMENT** of these new communities exhibited extremely high satisfaction and identity with the community and the neighborhoods, or "villages" as they were typically called, that made up the overall community. The villages varied in size but usually contained a number of housing types, schools, parks, identity amenities, and neighborhood-serving commercial development.

■ **COSTS FOR INFRASTRUCTURE** in the new communities ranked them among the most efficient development categories in the "costs of sprawl" studies of the 1970s.

In summary, Forsyth believes that planned communities of the 1960s and 1970s are not the development dinosaurs of a previous age; they are pioneers of urban design and planning strategies that are relevant today. They have a great deal to teach current developers of new urbanist projects and projects based on smart growth principles.

DEFINING THE FUTURE OF SMART GROWTH IN THE SUBURBS

The key questions for the future are (a) how much new growth can be expected in coming decades and (b) where can it reasonably be accommodated. In a 2010 book, *The Next Hundred Million: America in 2050*, urban scholar Joel Kotkin predicts that massive development to accommodate the expected population growth will reenergize and diversify America and its suburbs, where he believes much of that growth will occur. Some advocates of smart growth see growth accommodated primarily as urban infill. Infill development has many advantages, but it cannot fully accommodate the kind of 21st-century growth foreseen by Kotkin and projected by the U.S. Census Bureau.

OPPOSITE **Weston Town Center, Florida;** ABOVE **Entrance to the Islands of Cocoplum, Coral Gables, Florida.**

One answer to the question of where this massive growth will occur is found in a 2010 study by the U.S. Environmental Protection Agency, *Residential Construction Trends in America's Metropolitan Regions*. The study states, "Although urban core neighborhoods have doubled or tripled their share of residential construction since the early 1990s, they still account for less than half of all new residential units in most regions.

>>> funds to support the development company and allowed the communities to improve despite the downturn.

"Chuck approaches each resort as if it is one of his children, each with his or her own attributes. Chuck does not have a cookie-cutter formula ... he reinvents all the time. He takes the time to carefully craft each strategy. He cringes when people talk about development of a project in a vacuum. He thinks long term—sustainable in the largest sense. The number-one issue in second-home communities is not the initial cost of purchasing but the total cost of ownership. We have made a real drive to keep those costs reasonable and are at the forefront of that issue. For example, our clubs are inclusionary, and we find creative ways to reduce direct dues and assessments by including revenue sources such as local sales tax and transfer fees to support community and club services. Our clubs encourage the social interactions that create community. Kids meet on the mountain, then their families start mountain biking or skiing together. This process accelerates their comfort level and makes them feel part of the community faster."

Gary Engle joined Arvida in 1980 to work on the company's strategic plan. He left in 1987 to form Cobb Partners and stayed until 1990, but has continued his involvement with the Cobb Web to the present as a partner and investor in Kirkwood and Durango. His take is, "Arvida had a very big edge, because we had a lot of land with low land base, and we could afford to do it right. I was not big on curvilinear streets and culs-de-sac. But the Arvida products were not only attractive when we sold, they promised to age well. Royal Palm is an example of building around the Boca hotel, using the Mizner touches, including streetscape, lots of value. Boca West tried to create the value at a greater magnitude than anything before. Streets, landscaping, nothing special about the housing at first. When you start a project like that and get a front end, a certain market comes in; it's hard to mess it up.

"The good thing about Arvida, aside from reasonable discipline about design and landscaping, is that we never put ourselves in financial harm's way. We never had to distress any real estate; we got our price point. We were good on the design side, but where we were really good, was we really understood how to make money—the culture kept financial discipline, yet entrepreneurial opportunities. If we had stayed at Arvida after 1987, I am sure that we would have incorporated new urbanism into our communities. I developed a new urbanist project for Cobb Partners in South Beach and then for my own account called Kettle Valley in British Columbia." >>>

The 'urban infill' share would be larger if redevelopment in growing suburbs was also considered, but it would still not likely represent a majority of new construction in more than a handful of regions" (p. 20). Even in metropolitan areas such as Washington, D.C., and Portland, Oregon, that encourage infill development, such development is expected to accommodate only a minor portion of all new growth. Therefore, if at least half of all new growth in most American communities will occur in the outlying areas, the question is how to ensure that it is compact, sustainable, smart growth.

In a 2004 Urban Land Institute working paper, *Greenfield Development without Sprawl: The Role of Planned Communities*, Jim Heid offers one solution to this essential, outlying component of growth. He states, "Smart growth is an idea that captures the imagination, but lacks definitive implementation tools. Planned communities are a proven tool that is already playing a significant role in balancing the challenges of preventing sprawl, while creating high-quality living environments in greenfield areas" (p. 24). He suggests a state and local process that would discourage planned-unit developments that are just "subdivisions on steroids" but would encourage any new growth that needs to occur in outlying or greenfield areas to be made up of master-planned communities that address the evolving smart growth principles.

ABOVE Entry topiary at Sawgrass, near Jacksonville, Florida.

CHARACTERIZING THE MASTER-PLANNED COMMUNITIES OF CHUCK COBB

The master-planned communities that were developed by Chuck Cobb from the 1960s to the 1990s were different from the urban sprawl that pervaded that period of American development in the following ways:

- **THEY HAD A BALANCED MIX** of land uses that included a variety of housing types, employment centers, shopping, civic and educational facilities, and diverse kinds of recreation appropriate to their size and location.

- **THE LARGER COMMUNITIES** included jobs, housing, shopping, and community facilities in proximity.

- **THEY PROVIDED SITES** for schools; parks; churches; and other civic, cultural, and community institutions within or close to neighborhoods.

- **THEY PROVIDED INFRASTRUCTURE** for transportation, security, utilities, and services, with mechanisms to finance and maintain them.

- **THEY INCLUDED LARGE AREAS** of recreational or passive open space, environmental preserves, and water management areas.

- **THEY WERE PLACES TO LIVE, WORK, AND SHOP** that encouraged a rich variety of community and recreational experiences through clubs and community associations.

- **THEY WERE QUALITY CONTROLLED** by the master developer who set up design guidelines, homeowners associations, and special districts to ensure continuity of governance beyond the buildout period.

- **THEY HAD A COMPREHENSIVE PLAN** that featured a distinctive and complete image-setting landscape for all streets, entries, waterways, natural features, villages, business and commercial centers, and recreational amenities.

- **FINALLY, THEY WERE ORGANIZED,** managed, and marketed as communities, not as separate real estate subdivisions, business parks, or shopping centers.

Because of these features and characteristics, the master-planned communities that are described in this book offer some lessons for those planning and developing tomorrow's communities. In particular, they provide examples of the role privately financed and developed master-planned communities can play in this future and how they can adapt to the new urgencies of green and sustainable development.

>>> Peter Rummell has a unique view of the Cobb Web, coming from his experience at Charles E. Fraser's Sea Pines "University" and the Ocean Reef Club to work with Arvida in 1977 at Sawgrass in Jacksonville. He saw the Cobb Web in operation in Boca Raton and again at Disney Development, and took these and other real estate experiences to shape a career as one of the most creative and successful community developers in the country. In his words, "I am the sum of the parts. I came to Jacksonville just as Sawgrass was being bought from bankruptcy from the then Atlantic Bank. We had to get it jump-started; we created a sales team. The Cobb Web was the Arvida support group in Boca Raton. We did things more creatively, more about vertical product because the master plan with the golf course, the club, and the roads was very set. We had those constraints, but we had good land, a good location on the beach. Jacksonville and the beaches are now joined at the hip, but 35 years ago they were very separate places. Now it is a first-home place because of the major expressway that was built, that we made happen.

"Buying Arvida was meant to jump-start Disney real estate. Arvida ran Arvida while the new entity [Disney Development] ran Disney real estate, and Chuck oversaw the combined entity. Chuck sent me there. We brought a more structured process for ideas, a level of outside process to the effort—a net add. Several years later, after Cobb was gone, I ran what became known as Disney Development, and it was merged with Imagineering. Imagineering was creative place-making, so I ran the combined corporation. Celebration, the only community development by Disney, was done after the Arvida era."

The Cobb Web was a financially disciplined system that allowed individual creativity and entrepreneurship, as is made apparent from these comments and from experiencing the communities that were built under this unique system. It came from a clear understanding that creating great communities took the utmost and best efforts of many talented people. The Cobb Web name came not from the "sticky" web of a spider but from the complexity of relationships that made such communities possible. It remained flexible so that many of the best and brightest could sustain long careers in the Cobb Web and in later years have developments of their own, such as Temple and Zohn. Others would leave the Cobb Web and move on to other successful careers, as Rummell did at Disney and St. Joe or Rick Miller did in leading Fortune 500 companies after his key role in building Arvida's communities at Boca Raton. Anyone taking on the considerable task of building communities today can benefit from the experiences of this remarkable and resilient system.

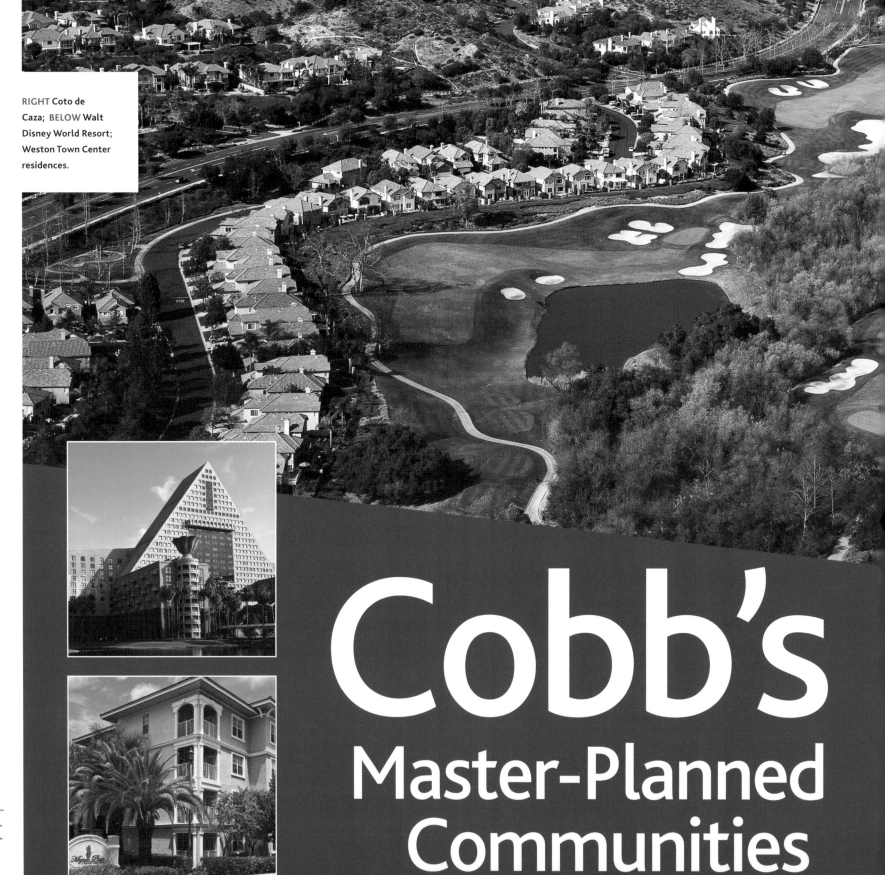

Cobb's
Master-Planned
Communities

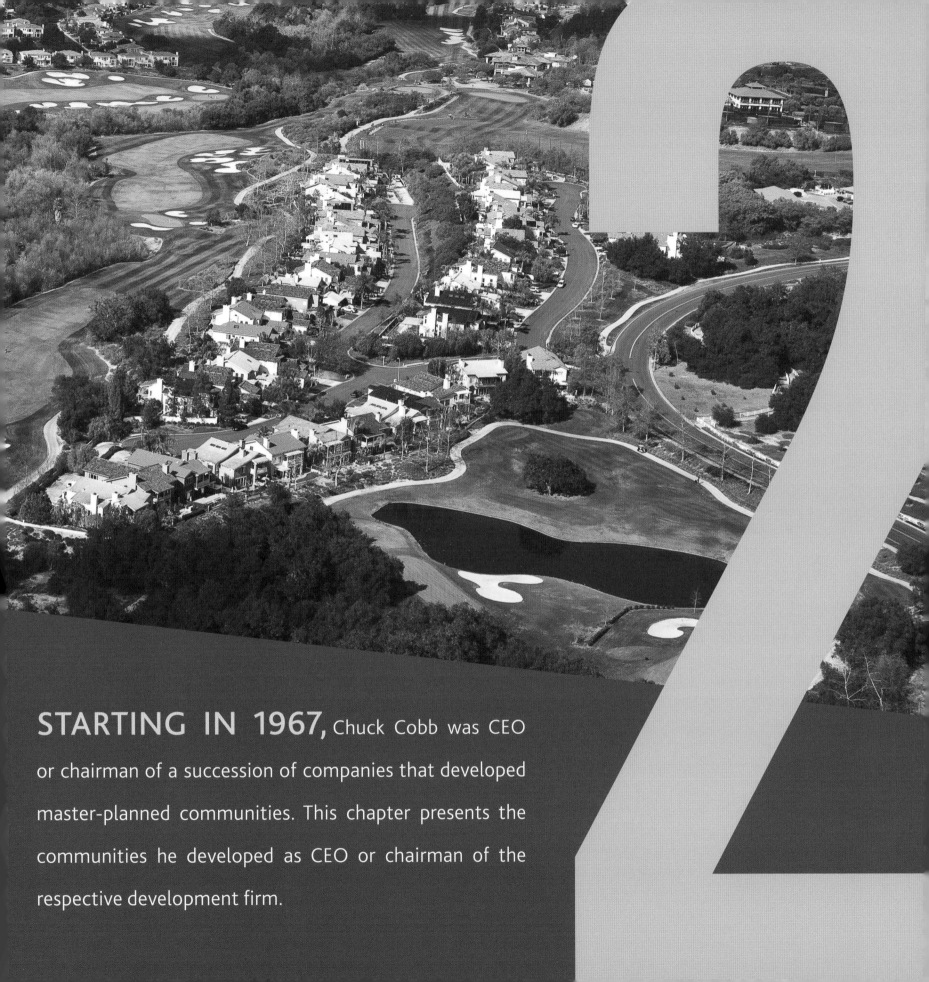

STARTING IN 1967, Chuck Cobb was CEO or chairman of a succession of companies that developed master-planned communities. This chapter presents the communities he developed as CEO or chairman of the respective development firm.

Rancho California

TEMECULA AND RIVERSIDE COUNTY, CALIFORNIA
A 95,000-acre master-planned community | **KAISER AETNA, 1964**

Starting in 1964, when he was chief financial officer of Kaiser Aluminum's real estate companies, Chuck Cobb worked out the financing and purchase of the 95,000-acre Vail cattle ranch located 90 miles southeast of Los Angeles and 60 miles north of San Diego that would become Rancho California. Over the next few years, intensive master planning was begun, and some strategic large tracts of land were sold to local farmers for exclusive use as citrus and avocado orchards and vineyards, setting the tone of the 148-square-mile ranch as a "country community." In 1967, Cobb was given the responsibility at Kaiser for Rancho California, and in 1969, when Kaiser merged its real estate activities with those of Aetna Life Insurance, he became group executive in charge of all Kaiser Aetna's large-scale master-planned communities in California and Arizona.

The late 1960s and subsequent years saw incredible growth and development in the Los Angeles metropolitan area, but much of that growth was a sprawl of scattered subdivisions replacing agricultural lands with a resulting lack of adequate infrastructure or sense of community, creating multiple kinds of environmental damage. With the ability to assemble multiple community-sized tracts of land and to plan, organize, and build out those properties to fit the land and people's diverse needs, Cobb, as head of Kaiser Aetna's development division, believed the company could give people better choices of where to live, work, shop, learn, and play while still protecting the natural environment and the agricultural heritage of California.

One important way that master-planned communities such as Rancho California were pioneers was their allocation of permanent open space. Standard suburbia—a patchwork quilt, where the land is a jumble of developed and undeveloped land with inefficient infrastructure—does not offer decent open space for residents' use and does not provide large enough areas to support wildlife or native flora. In master-planned communities, however, large and contiguous areas of open space are set aside to maximize their value for nearby residents, complement the built infrastructure, and protect original environmental characteristics such as water flow

OPPOSITE An overview of Temecula in central Rancho California; TOP TO BOTTOM An equestrian at the Santa Rosa Estates to the west of Temecula; Abbott Vascular Laboratories' new Temecula facility; Promenade Mall in Temecula.

and wildlife habitats. Such protected land, which boosts the value of nearby properties, requires careful analysis of land and natural resources to achieve a practical and sustainable size and configuration.

THE RANCHO CALIFORNIA CONCEPT

The overall policy for developing Rancho California was to accommodate growth without destroying the productive agricultural base. Open range would become farmland in a planned, orderly manner and then would be capable of absorbing urban and industrial needs gracefully without destroying the beauty or productivity of the land.

The first planners hired by Kaiser in the mid-1960s to address the future development had experience in the early planning of the Irvine Ranch in nearby Orange County and Valencia at the Newhall Ranch in Los Angeles County. They included Jack Bevash, who was a planner at Irvine; Victor Gruen, planner for Valencia; and Sasaki, Walker Associates, which was also working at both of those communities.

Headed by Cobb, the management team worked with these and other consultants to set the vision of the Rancho California community: to create an urban community with an encompassing greenbelt of open space and protected agriculture. Almost five decades later, the master plan vision and guidelines of dividing the community into 20 percent urban and 80 percent rural have produced the thriving, well-balanced city of Temecula and the surrounding Riverside County agricultural and estate areas.

With a population of more than 110,000 and more than 35,000 jobs, Temecula is concentrated in a clearly bounded, compact, and centrally located portion of the original Rancho California Plan that is designated for industrial, commercial, and residential community uses on both sides of Interstate 15. The city is framed on the east and west by the remaining 80 percent of the Rancho California planned community, which successfully blends ranches and rural estates with carefully protected agriculture, open space, recreation, and environmental preserves.

The Rancho California Water District, which was formed and initially operated by Kaiser Aetna, is now a highly capable public district covering all of the original 95,000-acre property, including the city of Temecula. It supplies water for all city, agricultural, and fire protection needs, and it maintains the sewer system for urban portions of the community. In the early days, the orientation of the district, which the master developer controlled, was to plan for the future. Therefore, as one former board member said during a visit in 2010, "If we needed a 12-inch line then, we put in a 36-inch line for the future, and this foresight has really paid off. Having a dependable source of water was key to having the right mix of residential and agriculture endure, as it has for all these years."

RIGHT Central Temecula with the Santa Rosa Plateau in the distance.

THE CITY OF TEMECULA: URBAN RANCHO CALIFORNIA

The introduction to the Temecula General Plan states: "In 1964, Kaiser Aluminum and Chemical purchased Vail Ranch, to begin Temecula's transition from avocado orchards, vineyards and other agricultural uses, to an urbanized community by preparing the Rancho California Development Plan. The overall land use pattern and circulation system of Temecula today has largely been guided by this plan. In 1989, Temecula incorporated [approximately 19 percent of Rancho California] as a General Law City"; it has recently grown to about 20 percent of the original ranch.

One of the cornerstones of Temecula's success as an exceptionally well-run city—with no debt and a solid tax base—is Kaiser Aetna's early planning and marketing to bring job-producing commercial and industrial development, not just residences, to Rancho California. Kaiser Aetna agreed to donate the right-of-way for the planned I-15 freeway to accelerate its completion. Within a few years, the industrial park boasted more than 2,000 jobs. Abbott Vascular, which for many years has been one of the area's largest employers, attests

to the continuity of this attraction with its new research and development (R&D) and manufacturing facility, substantially increasing its employment to a total of 5,000 employees in 2010.

Commercial development in Temecula includes well-landscaped and design-controlled business and industrial parks, easily accessible shopping districts, and Old Town. The Old Town district, which consisted of 400 people and a few businesses dating back to the 1890s, was included in the Rancho California plan and water district. Over the past decades, the area has been discovered by visitors to the Temecula wine country, and it has been rejuvenated and enlarged as a mixed-use historic district. The city is building its new civic center in Old Town, closing the loop on its history. At the Promenade Mall, the latest additions feature street-side businesses and parking, and walkable outdoor shopping and entertainment areas.

The city provides full services, including the library, a museum, and the Temecula Unified School District. The community includes seven small private institutes of higher learning. A task force is underway to plan

ABOVE The village of Harveston in Temecula; **LEFT** Housing in Harveston Village.

the transformation of the small outreach campus of California State University San Marcos at Temecula into a full-fledged campus.

The city followed the plan's original idea of a series of villages containing schools and parks connected by well-landscaped streets and a network of "natural stormwater washes" or green drainage ways that connect parks and open spaces. The development of Temecula's neighborhoods has evolved from the planned unit developments (PUDs) and golf communities of the 1970s and 1980s to the newest neighborhood, Harveston, built by Lennar in the 21st century. The Harveston neighborhood has more intimately mixed housing types and enhanced walkability around a central lake and greenways.

Of the 35,000 dwelling units in the city, 64 percent are lower-density single-family and 36 percent are higher-density (12 to 20 dwelling units per acre) multifamily units. When first developed as a part of Rancho California, the city of Temecula was considered affordable, particularly compared to adjacent Orange and San Diego counties. The focus on planned infrastructure, nearby jobs, a high level of amenities, and development controls in the city and throughout Rancho California created a desirable market that pushed prices higher than in other parts of Riverside County and to closer parity with the surrounding coastal counties.

ABOVE A playing field in the village; OPPOSITE Homes in Old Town Temecula.

In 2009, the Riverside Transit Agency initiated two free trolley routes connecting Old Town, the proposed bus transit center, the Promenade Mall, Harveston, and the farmers market. With its proposed line along I-15, the California high-speed rail project has one of its 26 statewide stations at Murrieta-Temecula with a loop connection to the Temecula Transit Center.

THE RIVERSIDE COUNTY WESTERN PORTION OF RANCHO CALIFORNIA: THE SANTA ROSA PLATEAU

To the west of I-15, Rancho California Road climbs the 2,000-foot escarpment that forms the western edge of Temecula up to the 36,000-acre Santa Rosa Plateau. This rolling mountainous area was planned and developed in the 1970s into avocado and citrus groves mixed with ranch estates. Kaiser had an innovative program of financing and management tools so a small ranch estate of only several acres could count on having available professional maintenance and marketing for its trees and crops. Today, 40 years later, the area is still characterized by orchards climbing the hills interspersed with white fences defining the properties. Many ranch estates have equestrian facilities, and these, along with the orchards, the well-maintained roads, signage, fencing, and varied ranch homes, fit well into the natural mountain setting.

A second access up to the plateau is to the north from the adjacent city of Murrieta. This access is marked by the Bear Creek Golf Club, designed by Jack Nicklaus and now part of Murrieta. As an early part of Rancho California, Bear Creek leads up to the 8,200-acre Santa Rosa Plateau Ecological Reserve. A protected area in the Riverside County Southwest Area Plan, this plateau includes historic sites, critical habitats, and exceptional vernal pools. The policy for the large Santa Rosa Plateau areas of ranch estates and agriculture that surround the reserve is to maintain the rural and natural character of the area.

THE RIVERSIDE COUNTY EASTERN PORTION OF RANCHO CALIFORNIA: WINE COUNTRY, EQUESTRIAN AND RECREATION AREAS

The areas that border the east boundary of Temecula that were part of the Rancho California planned community were planted with grapevines in the 1970s after the University of California, Davis, deemed the land "superior" for growing premium wine grapes. Today, the area has 35 wineries with public tasting rooms and other wine-country facilities that make it one of the largest and most successful wine regions in the state.

Amberton

VENTURA COUNTY, CALIFORNIA | KAISER AETNA, 1969

AS RANCHO CALIFORNIA BEGAN INTENSIVE DEVELOPMENT in the early 1970s, Kaiser Aetna purchased 10,000 acres in the Las Posas Valley of Ventura County, California, to plan a community in this agricultural valley 50 miles northwest of Los Angeles that would echo the successful approach at Rancho California. The first phase of the Rancho Ventura, or Amberton, community was planned as avocado estates from two to 20 acres in size, professionally managed for the homeowners. The next phases would be residential villages, a college village, commercial agriculture, a regional center, and multiuse recreation.

Kaiser sold a 425-acre portion of the site to the state for a potential state college to be located along a section of the proposed Simi Freeway traversing the valley. The firm began development of the first 350-acre avocado estate subdivision and then applied to Ventura County for planned community approvals for the entire 10,000-acre property.

Environmental activists and local farming interests mounted a challenge to the extension of the freeway through the valley and to the planned community at Amberton. After a long and arduous process, the Las Posas portion of the Simi Freeway was canceled and the master plan for Amberton was not approved. The community and the college never materialized. Kaiser sold the acreage in small agricultural parcels, and the valley remains in agricultural use today. The current county plan designates the entire 10,000 acres in 40-acre minimum agricultural use or open space, with the exception of the first avocado estates area and a small preexisting rural village.

The Rancho California concept was well received and worked extremely well in one outlying county of metropolitan southern California. At Amberton, in a similar outlying location, stakeholders did not support a planned community, even of a lesser size than Rancho California, but favored continued small-scale agricultural activities with only limited rural community growth in existing towns. The opportunity for increased jobs, educational facilities, and varied housing and commercial development was lost. This was more a "no growth" than "smart growth" approach, but in both Rancho California and this part of Ventura County the favored concepts have been sustained over 40 years.

OPPOSITE An estate cluster on the Santa Rosa Plateau overlooking Temecula; **LEFT** Old street trees and white fences on the Plateau.

The Riverside County plan covers this area with the 7,500-acre Citrus Vineyard Rural Policy Area and Citrus/Vineyard Zone protecting the rural and agricultural character.

A thoroughbred horse-breeding and training area was developed early at Rancho California next to the vineyard area. It includes the Galway Downs track and several large equestrian facilities surrounded by horse ranches of 10 acres at minimum. This area is protected by the 3,000-acre Valle de los Caballos Policy Area in the county plan. This relatively flat and gentle rolling grasslands area faces pressure to reduce the lot sizes below 10 acres but continues to have strong community support even in the face of the increasing cost of keeping horses.

One major feature that was not foreseen in the Rancho California plan was development on and adjacent to the Pechanga Indian Reservation to the south of the planned community. With the advent of gaming on Indian lands, the Pechanga Resort and Casino became the largest employer in the area. The casino is well positioned adjacent to the golf course and inn that were part of the first phase of development on the ranch.

Vail Lake at the southeast corner of the Rancho California Planned Community was built by the Vail family for their large cattle ranch before they sold the property to Kaiser. It serves as a reservoir for the water district but is still privately owned. In the Rancho California Plan, the lake was designated and developed for sailing and recreational fishing with a small area for camping and recreational vehicles at one edge. The 1970 Kaiser-Aetna Progress Report establishes "the necessity for preserving the integrity of resources such as 850-acre Vail Lake and its surrounding 8,000 acres," which is reflected in the current Riverside County 8,000-acre Vail Lake Policy Area that protects its biological resources and open space and limits development to the current recreational use areas.

RANCHO CALIFORNIA AFTER 40 YEARS

Rancho California planned for and has created a vital region of southern California. Four decades after its inception, it includes the robust and compact city of Temecula with a balanced mix of land uses, surrounded by large agricultural and estate areas, celebrated wine country, and open spaces and environmental preserves. It has provided a vibrant and sustainable economic base of jobs and businesses as well as a variety of housing and community uses. Current city and county plans closely follow the Rancho California Development Plan and provide citizen-based validation of this master-planned community's continuing desirability and community livability.

Chuck Cobb proudly describes this community as "one of the most satisfying and successful new towns for which I had responsibility."

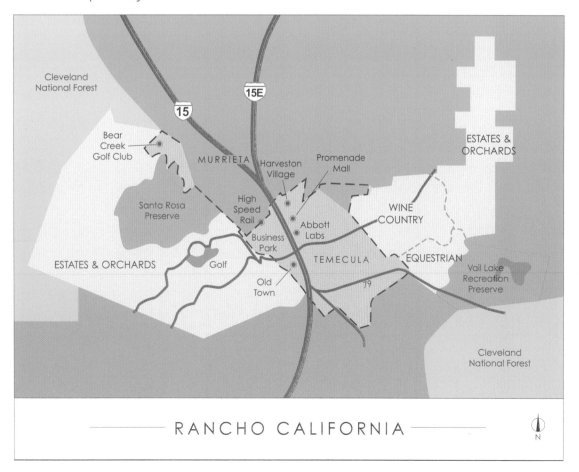

RANCHO CALIFORNIA

McCormick Ranch

In 1969, Chuck Cobb, John Temple, and their team at Kaiser Aetna purchased the 4,235-acre McCormick Ranch in Scottsdale, Arizona, for $11 million, or $2,800 per acre. It was the largest single property in the city at that time and Scottsdale's first master-planned community. Gruen Associates prepared the master plan for the entire ranch with the assistance of Scottsdale's former chief city planner, George Fretz, as planning consultant to Kaiser Aetna. In 1971, the city granted approval for the first phase. Planning of the remaining land took another year, with some modifications in 1979 with the sale of the 1,119-acre eastern portion of the master plan to another developer as the Scottsdale Ranch.

The master plan contained two then-novel features. Before this time, most of the infrastructure in Scottsdale was built using public funds, bonds, and local improvement districts. McCormick Ranch was the first development to build or contribute significantly to its major infrastructure without specific conditions of that sort imposed by the city. The Scottsdale General Plan of 2001 acknowledges that "this project would inspire many subsequent developments throughout the Phoenix metropolitan area. With the advent of master-planned development came new concepts and policies such as developer-built public improvements, contributions to the infrastructure, and amenities to support the newly created neighborhoods."

McCormick Ranch's other planning advance was its various physical, functional, and visual connections to surrounding Scottsdale. The developed property was not designed to be an isolated island that was intentionally separate from the rest of Scottsdale. Connections were achieved by continuing the green areas and drainage facilities of the Indian Bend Wash that traverses Scottsdale into the ranch, by extending Scottsdale's major street network into the ranch, and by creating a balanced mix of land uses and neighborhoods in the ranch. The two sections of McCormick Ranch are defined by Pima Road, a major north-south road that follows the edge of the Pima Indian Reservation. In recent years, Pima Road has been transformed into a major freeway, but the two communities continue to be strongly connected by the grade-separated vehicular and pedestrian spines in the original plan.

RIGHT A morning jog at the ranch; OPPOSITE TOP Bicycling lakeside on the walk; Scottsdale Road Bridge over Indian Bend Wash at Camelback Lake; neighborhood shops at McCormick Ranch.

Today, the Ranch has been fully developed in two sections: 3,116 acres with 23,000 residents under the McCormick Ranch Property Owners Association and the 1,119-acre eastern portion with 8,500 residents under the Scottsdale Ranch Community Association. The approximate total population of 31,500 for the ranch is 10 percent less than the original estimate of 35,000 because of the smaller household sizes of the older families the community attracted. The development followed the plan in providing its share of jobs, commercial facilities, and recreational amenities throughout the community.

McCORMICK RANCH COMMUNITY

The southern section of McCormick Ranch comprises recreation-based neighborhoods planned around two golf courses, a series of lakes, and Indian Bend Wash, the continuation of the major north-south drainage greenway that runs through Scottsdale. The largest lake, Camelback Lake, is adjacent to Scottsdale Road in the part of the ranch where Indian Bend Wash turns to the northwest and continues as a major drainage and greenway into adjacent Paradise Valley and then into the city of Phoenix.

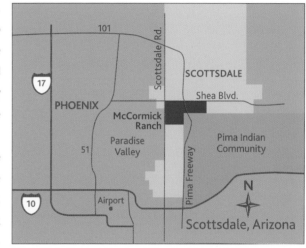

To extend the greenway amenity into the northern portions of the ranch beyond the point where Indian Bend Wash left the city, the master plan created the Camelback Walk Greenway. This linear park follows the smaller natural washes that extend north from Indian Bend and serves a critical hydrological function. It is a 3.5-mile-long grade-separated bicycle and pedestrian way that extends from Camelback Lake on the south and continues along the golf courses, lakes, parks, and neighborhoods through the entire McCormick Ranch Community.

Camelback Walk then continues under the Pima Freeway to the Scottsdale Ranch Community and ends at the major commercial and health centers along Shea Boulevard. It is a well-used recreational amenity that reduces pedestrian conflicts with vehicles moving through the community. It is used by children bicycling to school or parks and by adults bicycling, jogging, and walking with neighbors and families.

LEFT View from the ranch toward Camelback Mountain with Phoenix to the right of the mountain and Scottsdale to the left.

Hayden Parkway was planned and built as a lushly landscaped north-south road through McCormick Ranch, connecting neighborhoods and business districts along its length. The residential neighborhoods include a wide range of housing types from single-family lakefront and golf course homes to attached villas, townhouses, and a variety of multifamily condominiums. The housing mix responded to market conditions over the development period. Parks, schools, recreation, and community centers follow along Camelback Walk, and a series of smaller greenways thread throughout the neighborhoods and connect them to Hayden Parkway, Camelback Walk, schools, shopping, and recreational facilities.

Underpass at
Camelback Walk
allows automobile-
free pedestrian
circulation.

Resort hotels at McCormick Ranch are located along the Scottsdale Road Resort Corridor and adjacent to the golf course. Business parks with office buildings and neighborhood shopping centers occupy several locations along Hayden Parkway.

SCOTTSDALE RANCH COMMUNITY

Kaiser sold the northeastern section of the McCormick Ranch to another developer after the master plan was approved, and that section was developed as Scottsdale Ranch. It was planned for an older demographic than the southern section of the ranch, anticipated to possibly feature a retirement community and a health center. In fact, both the McCormick Ranch and Scottsdale Ranch segments of the master-planned community were largely occupied by older residents, which reduced the need for schools but increased the desirability of a major health center. This demographic trend has continued to the present.

The western third of Scottsdale Ranch was designated in the master plan as the McCormick Ranch Center for a major region-serving multiuse complex including business, commercial, industrial, and civic uses. It now houses the Scottsdale Healthcare campus, a major regional medical facility. It also accommodates shopping, industrial, and office uses that serve the larger area.

The residential areas to the east along Shea Road are built around the large-fingered Lake Serena and the 42-acre Scottsdale Ranch Park, which includes a school, a Boys and Girls Club, a desert garden, and the Scottsdale Senior Center. The homes are more modest in character and price than in most parts of the

ABOVE An office building along Scottsdale Road; **RIGHT** Boats on Lake Serena at the Scottsdale Ranch.

southern section. These neighborhoods consist of single-family dwellings, villas, patio homes, townhouses, and some apartments.

AN EVOLVING MARKETPLACE

Because it was planned and built four decades ago, McCormick Ranch has made various adjustments in response to changing market forces, which show how master-planned communities can successfully age with

time in terms of appearance, features, and market values. McCormick Ranch has become one of those communities that have the location and amenities needed to hold value and desirability over time. Homes and businesses are continuously upgraded and maintained, as are the common facilities and amenities, unlike small subdivisions where such improvements or long-term investments are unlikely or sporadic.

Because McCormick Ranch was planned in 1970–1971 and its first communities went onto the market then, both its master plan and the product mix at various locations have been altered over time in response to changing consumer demand and trends.

As an example of how the master plan adapted to market changes, an equestrian-oriented neighborhood with a series of riding trails was originally planned in an area along Hayden Parkway in the northwest portion of the property. When the neighborhood was built, the market and existing residents favored a more traditional residential neighborhood. So the trails were made into a network of pedestrian and bicycle greenways, and homes were built and successfully sold in this attractive environment.

Another change from the plan was the building of fewer, larger schools rather than the small schools that were called for because of modified school board policies and reduced need, given that many households at McCormick Ranch did not have school-age children. However, the master plan basics of land uses, unit mix, open space and drainage, and circulation were unchanged or modified in minor ways to adapt to Scottsdale growth.

A STRONG SENSE OF COMMUNITY

All of the residents, businesses, and institutions in McCormick Ranch have a sense of being part of the city of Scottsdale, which over time has expanded well to the north and east of the ranch. The city, which boasts high-quality neighborhoods, a well-known historic downtown, and a tradition of community involvement, good schools, parks, safety, and public services, is considered very desirable within the Phoenix metropolitan region. Scottsdale is now larger than 185 square miles, including 30 percent, or 56 square miles, in open-space preservation areas, and it has an estimated population of 300,000.

The residents and businesses of McCormick Ranch are not only part of this desirable city, but they also have an added sense of belonging from being part of a master-planned community. This community today is a good

example of how master planning and controlled development can provide long-term benefits to residents even within a well-run, established city. By planning and creating desirable infrastructure and patterns of lifestyles up front and by establishing two strong community associations with methods for facilitating and maintaining these lifestyles and the amenities that support them, the residents and businesses have additional layers that enhance the quality of their community.

OPPOSITE
Residents on
Camelback Walk;
LEFT Looking
north over Hayden
Parkway.

This was not lost on the city fathers of Scottsdale in their long-term effort to create a great city. McCormick Ranch showed the value of master-planned communities and set a high standard for future developments. Significantly, much of the growth in Scottsdale since the McCormick Ranch has been in planned communities. What has been accomplished here is well stated in the preface to the original 1971 Master Plan: "The essence of the plan is to afford opportunities for work and play: to relax, to shop, to earn a living, and to bring up one's family. This within a community large enough to satisfy most desires for enjoyment, for intellectual stimulus, for companionship, but without most of the burdens of urban life."

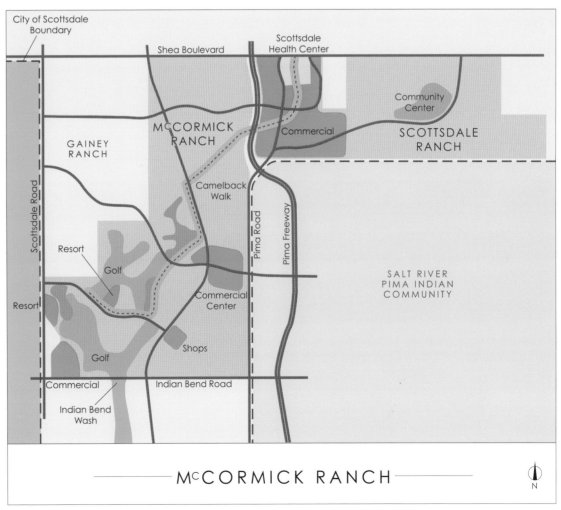

McCORMICK RANCH

Arvida at Boca Raton

In 1972, Chuck Cobb left Kaiser Aetna in California for the Arvida Corporation in Florida, which was founded by Arthur Vining Davis and others. In 1958, Arvida became a public company owned by Davis and other shareholders. Upon Davis's death in 1962, a controlling interest in Arvida was sold to a company that later became part of Penn Central, the railroad conglomerate. Davis had accumulated vast real estate holdings throughout Florida (including the Boca Raton Hotel and Club) but carried out only a few small land sales and developments on these properties. In 1972, the publicly held Arvida Corporation hired Chuck Cobb as its CEO to revitalize these holdings and to create the "new Arvida."

OPPOSITE TOP **The historic Cloisters Inn portion of the hotel; the trail systems at Broken Sound; Les Jardins village at Boca Raton;** LEFT **Single-family homes in a Boca West village.**

Given his success at Rancho California and McCormick Ranch in Arizona, Cobb not surprisingly chose to create multiple master-planned communities to achieve the highest and best use of the company's large landholdings. He recognized that environmental, social, and political trends throughout the nation were adding complexity, time, and cost to the government regulatory processes, and he believed that planned communities were emerging as a more efficient and better way to use land than the conventional subdivision or parcel development. Enlightened consumers, Cobb realized, were seeking a better quality of life, and they increasingly looked to superior physical and social environments to satisfy their lifestyle expectations and create rising values for their homes. Cobb set out to create a company structure that would plan and develop high-quality planned communities in response to this consumer demand.

ARVIDA QUALITY

In 1972, Arvida Corporation, under Cobb as chairman and CEO and later with John Temple as president and chief operating officer, made a fundamental business change to develop comprehensively planned communities on all the company's large landholdings. Through the 1970s and early 1980s, they had more than 20 planned communities under development in Florida, Georgia, and California. Arvida patterned its planned communities in response to consumer desire. Top priority was given to the development of ecologically balanced communities, affording residents both natural and built amenities.

Eight common elements were designed to achieve consistency, value, and excellence in all Arvida communities:

- Resource management and energy conservation;
- Comprehensive plan and enhancement of natural features;
- Recreation facilities and resort and club operations;
- Community character and product diversity;
- Image-setting entryway and controlled access and security;
- Streets and landscapes, graphics and signs;
- Stewardship responsibility and community management; and
- Marketing and sales promotional events.

This new development approach and structure was first used in Arvida's 5,000-acre property in the western part of the city of Boca Raton, extending into Palm Beach County and the landmark pink Boca Raton Hotel and Club on Florida's Gold Coast. Boca Raton became an example of "Arvida quality," and it set the stage for the 1980s when the corporation's more than 20 master-planned communities under development each set its own particular high standards in south Florida, the Gulf Coast, and northern Florida.

BOCA RATON IS A SPECIAL PLACE

"I Am the Greatest Resort in the World, I Am Boca Raton, Fla."

—Mizner Development Corporation, 1925

The city of Boca Raton was incorporated in 1925 when Addison Mizner, an architect and developer, founded the Mizner Development Corporation and launched his audacious dream of transforming a small agricultural community into the "Greatest Resort in the World—a Few Years Hence." On Florida's Gold Coast, 30 miles south of Palm Beach and 45 miles north of Miami, Mizner planned and developed gracious tree-lined boulevards, the 100-room Cloister Inn (later the Boca Raton Hotel and Club), and 30 homes in the Floresta area.

Mizner used the dramatic Mediterranean architectural style that had won him acclaim and clients in the Palm Beaches. That first year, wealthy patrons wintered in Boca Raton, thereby giving the new community its early "greatness" and its unique identity.

Although a gifted architect and developer, Mizner's timing could have been better. In 1926, the Florida real estate boom was turning into a bust: banks were failing, and investors and homebuyers avoided Florida properties, regardless of how well located and planned they might be. That September, a powerful hurricane swept up the Florida coast, damaging Miami, Palm Beach, and Boca Raton. The following year, Mizner's development company went under, and development stalled throughout the Great Depression. The Boca Raton Hotel was converted into a training facility for military officers during World War II.

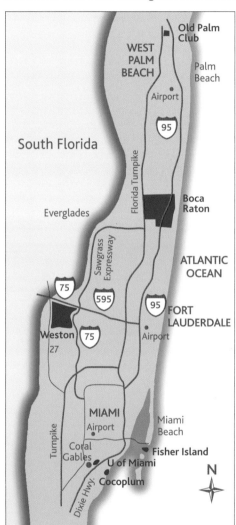

Arthur Vining Davis initiated the hotel's renaissance after he purchased it, along with other large real estate holdings, in the late 1950s. Directly across Camino Real from the Boca Raton Hotel, he developed the 500-acre private Royal Palm Yacht and Country Club with a yacht harbor and golf course designed by Robert Trent Jones, Sr. In 1962, Davis died at the age of 95, and for almost a decade, Arvida's management of existing properties and corporate ownership did not see any new large developments.

THE NEW ARVIDA AT BOCA RATON

In 1972, the new publicly held Arvida, under control by Penn Central with Chuck Cobb's leadership, began a comprehensive effort to plan for the future of the Boca Raton Hotel and Club, the Royal Palm enclave in the heart of Boca Raton, and the extensive 5,000 acres of properties located in western Boca Raton and Palm Beach County. Cobb wanted to recapture Addison Mizner's original vision of Boca Raton as a "special place" and to substantially increase the pace and scope that Arthur Vining Davis's few but important steps made toward that vision.

Arvida's new management team believed that these precedents could reestablish Boca Raton's special place and value in the fast-moving, formless suburban sprawl of south Florida growth that was advancing up the Gold Coast, a 70-mile-long series of subtropical beaches stretching from Miami to the Palm Beaches. Much of Boca Raton to the west of the hotel was still undeveloped. Arvida controlled a good portion of those lands and knew that the market existed for distinctive and high-quality development. In the early 1970s, large-scale planning decisions were imperative to Boca Raton's future because of the imminent completion of Interstate 95, connecting Boca Raton to Miami and Fort Lauderdale to the south and to the Palm Beaches to the north.

In 1972, Arvida presented a proposal to the city for a master-planned community with mixed uses and densities. The City Council quickly approved the plan, recognizing its suitability to expand the city as a "special place." But a group of citizens saw the plan another way and came forward with a 40,000-unit proposed cap on residential development in the city that would result in a low residential density overall to ensure only single-family uses would be allowed. The referendum was voted in and produced an arbitrary cap on all future development. Arvida initiated a series of lawsuits challenging the cap as arbitrary because the city had no comprehensive plan on which to justify that limit. Cobb feared the cap would not allow adequate flexibility to build diverse housing products to meet the various markets as they evolved and to create a complete community. Arvida went on to win each of the lawsuits, and in 1976, the cap was thrown out as arbitrary. However, the judge allowed the city to complete a new City Comprehensive Plan that in effect achieved the low-density goal without the cap.

Having spent $5 million and two years in litigation and recognizing that further legal appeals would just delay development on land in the city, Cobb and the team devised a strategy that would meet the low-density

LEFT The Beach Club with road and boat connections across Lake Boca Raton to the main hotel; **BELOW** The Arvida Tower and main hotel from Lake Boca Raton, and the Royal Palm Country Club to the left.

LEFT The entry to Boca West with the club center, golf courses, and villages; ABOVE Aquatics at the Boca West Country Club.

city plan and still allow the company to meet some of its long-term development and financial objectives. A large portion of the Arvida property was not located in the city of Boca Raton but in Palm Beach County, which had no development cap. On these lands adjacent to the city, Arvida sought, and Palm Beach County approved, a higher and more flexible set of densities. On the lands within the city of Boca Raton, Arvida would build the lower-density housing mandated by the city's plan as that market remained quite robust throughout the next decades.

BELOW One of Boca West's four golf courses; OPPOSITE Walkers in a Boca West village; a 1925 advertisement for Boca Raton.

On the positive side, a visionary group in the city started a City/South Palm Beach County Recreation District that produced a plan and raised the funds to acquire the several miles of Boca Raton's undeveloped beachfront. Before these properties could be lined with high-rise private development, a string of public parks, natural preserves, and beaches was established to assure its residents of permanent access to the marvelous beaches and oceanfront of the city.

CONNECTING THE VILLAGES OF ARVIDA TO THE "SPECIAL PLACE"

The SWA Group then prepared a coordinated city/county strategic plan for Arvida to allow the hotel and the extensive western properties to work closely together to meet the "special place" challenge. To achieve this goal, the plan first devised strategies to emphasize connections between the legendary Boca Raton Hotel and Club, marinas, and newly public beaches and the separate landlocked city and county lands, several miles to the west. Some of these new connections were physical, such as improved east-west circulation, whereas other connections were social, such as opening up hotel and club use to residents of all Arvida developments in the west. The hotel and club could benefit in turn from reciprocal arrangements with the new and under-used tennis facilities and golf courses in the Boca West Country Club Community, allowing hotel guests and club members access to these excellent facilities.

To strengthen the links between the various communities, the Boca Raton Hotel and Club shuttle buses carried people on a frequent east-west schedule to Boca West and its resort facilities. Arvida also funded an innovative program to provide a fully landscaped treatment to Florida State Road 808 (Glades Road), the city's major east-west arterial that connected the downtown to western Boca Raton, I-95, and the Florida Turnpike. For the first time in Florida history, a private company fully landscaped a state highway.

The Boca club's activities and the hotel's improved facilities provided prestige, identity, and real access to the Florida oceanfront and waterways for residents of all the Arvida Villages at Boca Raton. The purchase of an

Arvida home in Boca West or any other Arvida Village gave the owner the option of joining the club with different levels of access to its many facilities. This process continued over time, and as the Boca West Country Club facilities were taken over by the residents, a new championship golf course was built in the Arvida Park of Commerce to accommodate hotel and club members.

ARVIDA AS MASTER DEVELOPER

The plans that the SWA Group prepared at Boca Raton under the direction of Arvida drew upon these connection strategies and created a mixed-use master-planned community. It consisted of diverse residential villages, resorts, recreation, transportation and civic facilities, and commercial shopping and employment developments. These elements were then broken into components that could be processed as coordinated and linked PUDs or land subdivisions on the 5,000 acres to the west in the city and in the adjacent Palm Beach County areas controlled by Arvida.

This master-planned community was designed to complement the existing development within the city of Boca Raton, and as mentioned previously, would have particularly close functional connections and access to the planned enhancements of the legendary hotel and club property on the Boca Raton waterfront, such as the new Beach Club Hotel and the lakeside and golf course condominium villages. Developing a comprehensive planned community designed to fit into and complete a city with high-quality components throughout

was rare in Florida at the time, but the community did inherit some of its character from Cobb's work in doing exactly that several years earlier with Kaiser Aetna at the McCormick Ranch in Scottsdale, Arizona.

The basic building blocks of this plan were a highly diverse series of residential villages varying in size from about 100 to 300 homes. Each residential village had a distinctive character of design appropriate to its site and location and included landscaped roadways as well as pedestrian and bicycle trails. Landscaped entries and some combination of earthen berms or walls with thematic graphics became a unifying identity for all villages. The villages had internal amenities such as lakes, golf courses, parks, and school sites. Some of the villages were freestanding under the overall master plan, and others were part of larger city- or county-approved PUDs. These larger developments included the 1,400-acre Boca West Country Club with four golf courses, tennis, and spa, and 54 village clusters with 3,400 townhomes, villas, condominiums, and single-family home clusters. Near the town center was the 800-acre Via Verde villages with 3,700 townhouses, condominiums, and small-lot homes on a chain of lakes and greenways, and finally Broken Sound Country Club was a 1,000-acre family-oriented community of 3,000 primarily single-family houses on a golf course and lakes, with a tennis and spa center, and sites for an elementary school and a high school. Thus, a large and competitive diversity of housing products would be available in the overall community.

ABOVE Homes at Broken Sound Country Club; OPPOSITE The Broken Sound Country Club community.

Arvida played the role of master developer and provided the "horizontal development," including planning and government approvals, detailed land use, density and subdivision layouts, roads, water man-

agement, utilities, and design guidelines to maintain quality control. To ensure diverse product and still have builders with experience in the local markets, Arvida then developed a stable of builders from south Florida's best through an intensive interview and training process. Arvida was able to select the builders for all or part of each village using criteria established under a comprehensive marketing plan and to support the builders with an umbrella of the larger community marketing and communication programs. Arvida developed unique sports marketing programs on television, including national events such as the Pepsi Grand Slam and Virginia Slims tennis tournaments. These were used to promote the tennis and golf facilities and the communities at Boca Raton. It was one of the first uses of television in a real estate program in America, and it was a smashing success.

The commercial and industrial developments were planned as high-quality business parks or commercial centers with several coordinated elements to ensure they also contributed to the sense of a special place. They were key in creating the kind of employment that would be a good match for the housing in the villages. These developments included the Arvida Park of Commerce, an 810-acre planned business and industrial park development with a championship golf course, the first built in an industrial park in the United States.

The Executive Center, an 84-acre campus for offices around a central lake and park, along with the headquarter office sites around the Town Center, established Boca Raton as the primary office center in Palm Beach County. The Town Center with Neiman Marcus, Saks, Nordstrom, and Bloomingdale's department stores, as well as Macy's and Sears, added to the high-end but inclusive special place that was Boca Raton. The Town Center also had walkable commercial recreation centers and higher-density housing nearby. These larger commercial developments were region serving and therefore could be developed early on in conjunction with the residential villages, providing high standards of commercial service to new residents.

LEFT Pedestrians at Boca Center; ABOVE Homes on the greenway at Les Jardins.

Working with the Palm Beach County School Board, elementary, middle, and high schools were located on sites dedicated by Arvida. An institutional area with a series of religious complexes was designated along Yamato Road adjacent to Patch Reef Park. Arvida dedicated this 55-acre park with unique environmental characteristics to the city as well as several other smaller parks.

As the once-skeptical city officials and local residents saw the high quality of Arvida's developing communities, more frequent channels of communication opened. The two former opponents formed a working partnership to guide future development. The city added many of Arvida's planning, zoning, and development standards to its own codes, and many of Arvida's developments of varying densities in adjacent Palm Beach County were subsequently annexed to the city because of their overall quality.

BOCA RATON TODAY

In 1970, before the new Arvida plan, Boca Raton had approximately 30,000 residents and a small job base before IBM opened that year. By 2010, the city had almost 90,000 residents, and even with the dramatic reduction of IBM employees, the city has more than 90,000 jobs with a labor force of only 40,000. This surplus of employment contributed to a robust tax base for the city and included the opportunity for excellent jobs in technology and offices that matched well to the city's residents. Also, the location of these large employment facilities with direct access to I-95 and commuter rail buffered the community from congestion during commuting hours.

The city's density limits produced an imbalance in jobs and housing requiring workers to commute from other parts of the Gold Coast. It will continue to be difficult to provide enough affordable housing for all the jobs created by the Arvida planned community.

LEFT The Arvida Park of Commerce with the championship golf course; RIGHT Street landscaping and coordinated graphics at the Park of Commerce; an office building at the Park of Commerce.

The remarkable transformation of Boca Raton is largely owed to the Arvida developments described, which include a greatly enhanced hotel and club; diverse primary, retirement, and second homes; a new town center; and varied R&D, light manufacturing, office, and retail employment to create a community known throughout the country for its distinctive quality. At the peak of development, the hotel and club had 8,000 club members, and Boca West had 4,000. Most significant, the vibrant economy developed during this 40-year process, primarily through Arvida's efforts, enabled the citizens and the city to take bold steps to enhance the special place they desired by adding cultural and educational facilities, public beaches, and parks and by phasing the redevelopment of their downtown.

Chuck Cobb, as the leader of the new Arvida, built upon the visions of Addison Mizner and Arthur Vining Davis and was able to accomplish their dreams for Boca Raton as a special place.

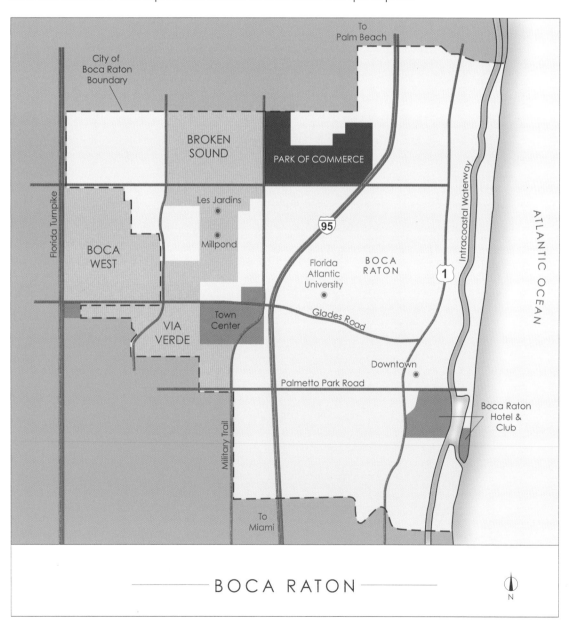

BOCA RATON

The bicycle trail at
Millpond Village.

Longboat Key Club

TOWN OF LONGBOAT KEY, SARASOTA COUNTY, FLORIDA
A master-planned community for Longboat Key | **ARVIDA CORPORATION, 1972**

Development on Longboat Key, the 10.8-mile-long barrier island on the Gulf Coast of Florida just off the coast of Sarasota, had a history of boom and bust with little planning or coordination. The beautiful pure white quartz sand beaches and frontage on Sarasota Bay had always attracted great interest, and in 1926 John Ringling of circus fame built a causeway 4.5 miles across the bay, connecting downtown Sarasota to the offshore keys. Ringling started development of the adjacent St. Armand's and Lido keys and began a luxury Ritz-Carlton Hotel on the south end of Longboat Key. The hotel was never finished, however, as the Florida boom and Ringling's fortunes came to an end in the late 1920s.

Three decades passed with no significant development. In fact, part of Longboat Key became a target range for Air Force pilots during World War II. After the war, demand for homes and condominiums on the island finally took root in the lots along Gulf of Mexico Drive down the center of the key, accessed from Bradenton Beach to the north and from the Ringling Causeway and Sarasota to the south. As the long key was divided in half by county jurisdictions—the north part in Manatee County and the south part in Sarasota County—the small group of residents wisely formed the town of Longboat Key in 1955 to provide unified governance.

In 1959, Arthur Vining Davis bought 1,100 acres on Longboat Key, which constituted the majority of the southern half of the town, and acquired the remaining undeveloped land on the adjacent keys. Arvida put its first emphasis on building out homes on the adjacent keys, then, in 1968, began development on Longboat Key with a Willard Byrd–designed golf course and parcels for residential development.

When Cobb arrived, he asked SWA Group to work on a second Willard Byrd golf course and to begin a master-planned community process for the entire 1,100 acres owned by Arvida. In 1976, Arvida secured approval from the town for two coordinated PUDs: the Islandside PUD on the Gulf of Mexico beachfront that included the existing golf course and the few developed beachfront projects, and the Harbourside PUD with a

RIGHT The Islandside community on the Gulf of Mexico; OPPOSITE TOP Single-family homes at Harbourside; the Islandside Tennis Center; the Gulf of Mexico beach at Islandside.

View from yacht club to boat harbor; OPPOSITE Path at Harbourside along boat channel and mangrove preserves.

new golf course and marina along Sarasota Bay. The two PUDs were designed to work together to create the Longboat Key Club resort community.

The plan also provided a new center for the town of Longboat Key. The 50-acre Town Plaza was planned by SWA Group to include the town hall, library, post office, banks, religious institutions, and Avenue of the Flowers Town Plaza. The site for the town plaza was densely covered with native oak trees, which provide an attractive setting for the center of this seaside town.

LONGBOAT KEY CLUB RESORT COMMUNITY

The Longboat Key Club comprises the two resort and recreational communities along the Gulf of Mexico beaches and Sarasota Bay, divided by the town plaza and the central town road, Gulf of Mexico Drive. Islandside, on the Gulf of Mexico beaches, was planned for 1,791 dwelling units on 380 acres in a series of mid-rise condominium villages, an 18-hole golf course, a 14-court tennis center, and a clubhouse. One of the condominium villages was situated on the site of Ringling's dream hotel and includes the 221-unit Inn on the Beach, a luxury resort accommodation. The beach at Islandside is for use by all residents and guests of that community.

Harbourside, along Sarasota Bay, is a lower-density community with 720 acres and 1,703 units, in a variety of single-family homes, town-

houses, and mid-rise and high-rise condominiums interspersed among the 18-hole golf course, 10 tennis courts, waterways, and open spaces. It includes a 277-slip marina with a yacht club, capacity to accommodate up to 60-foot boats, and a maintained channel connecting to the bay and the Intracoastal Waterway. A separate Beach Club is provided next to Islandside for use by the Harbourside residents.

Harbourside was designated as a wildlife refuge, so a channel was dug within the property boundaries along the entire bayfront perimeter, leaving a mangrove preserve between the channel and the waters of the bay. The channel and the mangroves were then deeded to the state of Florida. The town acquired the 45-acre Quick Point Nature Preserve at the southeastern tip of the key from Arvida. Approximately 50 percent of the Longboat Key Club land area is used for golf courses, waterways, and open-space preserves.

Longboat Key Club has bicycle and pedestrian paths to connect to the amenities and the town plaza. The town has extended these into an 11-mile bicycle and pedestrian way the entire length of the key. In recent years, a trolley service has been provided on the key, with connections to downtown Sarasota.

BELOW Harbourside community on Sarasota Bay with golf, yacht harbor, and mangrove preserves; **OPPOSITE** Mix of housing types at Harbourside.

Of particular concern in planning for the population of Longboat Key Club was evacuation during hurricane warnings. Studies were conducted to assess whether enough time and capacity existed for total evacuation of residents and visitors along the northern and southern routes, taking into consideration warning times and required bridge openings for marine traffic. Good planning required that a limit be placed on population for safety reasons.

TOWN OF LONGBOAT KEY

The long, thin barrier island, almost 11 miles long and one-half to one mile in width, had no center or civic focus until the town plaza was created as part of the planned community. Unlike the rest of the town, which was a linear mix of resort and residential uses strung somewhat haphazardly along Gulf of Mexico Drive, the planned community carefully related the resort and residential villages to the natural amenities of beach and bay and to new built amenities for golf, tennis, harbor, outdoor activities, and club functions. The plan had more dense uses directly related to beach, bay, harbor, and golf, and lower-density villages along the Harbourside waterways and extended golf links.

The goal was to attract visitors to the high-quality resort accommodations and to encourage guests to become residents by purchasing real estate. Much of this goal was achieved—especially in the markets for retirement homes and second homes for empty nesters. Indeed, in 2010, an estimated 12,000 of the town's population of 20,000, or 60 percent, were seasonal residents, and the average age was 66.

Harbourside was specifically planned at lower densities to attract families with children to provide diversity that would make up a true community. This goal would prove difficult to reach: the town had no significant jobs, and Sarasota is a retirement community with limited employment. Also, the key had no schools because the full-time resident population of the town was projected to be less than 8,000 at buildout, and the key was split into two counties and therefore two school districts.

ABOVE Longboat Key Town Hall at the Town Center; RIGHT The Inn at the Beach resort hotel at Islandside.

In 2010, the town had 6,000 condominiums, 2,000 single-family units, and 1,500 tourist rental units. In a visit to Longboat Key in 2010, Cobb was generally pleased with the outcome of the planned community. In a newspaper interview with the *Longboat Observer*, he said his only disappointments lie in the lack of families with children (3 percent in the 2000 census) and the lack of rentals to destination visitors that might bring more vitality and economic activity to the town. Some residents of the key share Cobb's desire for more families and tourists, and all want more retail activity and fewer vacant stores in the town plaza. However, in the town's 2007 Vision Plan, the idea of "Keeping Longboat, Longboat" reflects more of a "stay as we are" sentiment that is cautious about encouraging tourism. The consensus is that the only suitable tourist types are individuals, families, and business groups seeking a quiet and leisurely retreat.

RESORT COMMUNITY OR RECREATIONAL COMMUNITY?

Longboat Key is a prime example of the tension between destination resort and recreational community development. Through coordinated management, Cobb and Arvida were able to move Islandside more toward resort use for short-term, monthly, and seasonal guests and Harbourside more toward year-round residents. They could further minimize potential conflicts between the two categories of use by devising layers of clubs, marketing, and operations skills to successfully share the use of amenities in the two parts of the Longboat Key Club.

After buildout, when Arvida turned control over to the residents, community associations, and town, the measures built into the plan continued to provide means to accommodate both essential parts of the community. The question was whether these new owners had the desire to accommodate both forms of recreational use.

With its primary political interest in serving the residents, the town has a more difficult time providing balance between the resort and tourism aspects of the economy than would Arvida, whose incentive is to sell real estate. The town has enacted a series of policies to discourage tourism. Positioning Longboat as more of a destination resort would bring economic benefits, with more hotel, restaurant, and business activity. This increased activity would have to be balanced with any unwanted problems incurred by the town.

In summary, Arvida's vision was "Longboat Key Club, an Arvida Resort Community." The town of Longboat Key's vision is "Keep Longboat, Longboat." The first vision was to create the best kind of sustainable place to enjoy the beautiful natural setting of Longboat Key. The second vision is to keep the desirable place that was created and to protect that setting solely for the residents. To do so and still have viable local shops and businesses, the town will have to move beyond its resistance to becoming "too active" a tourist destination and define the meaning of "Keeping Longboat, Longboat" in less exclusionary terms. Cobb points to the proposed $400 million Islandside redevelopment plan and feels Longboat Key still has time to become a resort destination where the right kind of tourism can fit into the lifestyle so valued by the residents, yet still provide the continued vitality and means for a better life for everyone in the town.

OPPOSITE TOP Tree preservation at the town plaza parking areas; **LEFT** Shops and businesses on the Avenue of Flowers.

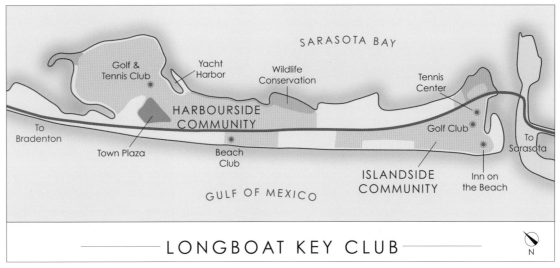

SARASOTA BAY

Golf & Tennis Club

Yacht Harbor

Wildlife Conservation

Tennis Center

HARBOURSIDE COMMUNITY

To Bradenton

Town Plaza

Beach Club

Golf Club

To Sarasota

ISLANDSIDE COMMUNITY

Inn on the Beach

GULF OF MEXICO

N

LONGBOAT KEY CLUB

RIGHT Main entrance to
Weston at Royal Palm
Boulevard; OPPOSITE
Golf at Weston Hills
Country Club; a café in
Weston Town Center.

Weston

Along with Rancho California, Cobb's other effort to plan and build a genuine new town from scratch is Weston, a master-planned community nine miles west of Fort Lauderdale. The 10,000-acre community, now the city of Weston, was begun in the mid-1970s when the convergence of three new major freeways was planned directly adjacent to the site, opening up excellent regional access to this last huge tract of developable urban land at the edge of the Everglades in Broward County.

Weston is defined on its east and north boundaries by I-75, which connected Florida's Gold Coast across the Everglades on "Alligator Alley" to the Gulf Coast cities of Naples, Fort Myers, Sarasota, and Tampa. Adjacent to the northeast corner of Weston, a large interchange with I-75 was planned to connect to the new I-595 that went directly east to the Florida Turnpike, I-95, Fort Lauderdale, and the recently expanded Fort Lauderdale International Airport. The interchange would also connect north to the planned Sawgrass Expressway, which skirted the edge of the Everglades and, in combination with I-75, was to provide an entirely new relief valve to the congested north-south corridors along the Gold Coast.

The site for Weston, therefore, would be directly connected by new freeways and expressways to Miami to the south, Fort Lauderdale to the east, Boca Raton and Palm Beach County to the north, and all of Gulf Coast Florida to the west. Few large parcels of developable Florida land could match this property in location and

opportunity, and Cobb took every measure to ensure that Weston would represent the highest standards of Arvida quality.

To the west of the Weston property were lands designated for nonurban uses, including Everglades conservation areas and some limited agricultural uses adjacent to U.S. Route 27. North of the property were

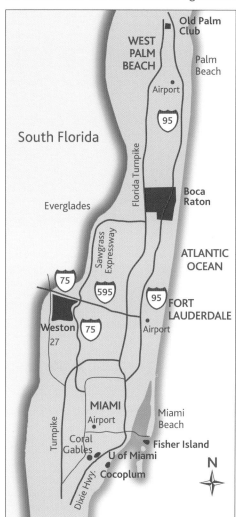

extensive south Florida regional water conservation areas and a large park. To the south along Griffin Road was an agricultural estate area, which, in 2000, became the town of Southwest Ranches, continuing to protect the rural lifestyle. All together, three edges of the Weston site would have no future urban development. The east boundary of the property was defined by the planned I-75, and from that edge of Weston were scattered subdivisions and commercial strips that sprawled across Broward County toward Fort Lauderdale and Hollywood on the coast. The development team recognized that this clearly defined and superbly accessed Weston property was perfectly suited to be a master-planned new town.

PLANNING A HOMETOWN

Arvida and the county needed to work together to evolve the planning to reflect the unique size, environment, location, and access of the site, and the Weston plan came under the new Florida law for large projects of regional impact. Cobb recognized the need to evolve the development approach for large projects beyond the customary days of boom and bust in Florida. In 1972, he was alone among CEOs of large real estate companies in supporting Governor Reubin Askew's landmark legislation to protect the state's areas of critical concern and to require all large development projects to complete an environmental and planning study called a Development of Regional Impact (DRI) before receiving the required approvals. These large projects and studies would go through an approval process that involved a specially designated regional agency set up by the state as well as the applicable local jurisdiction. Although this process would be more expensive and time consuming, Cobb could see the benefits from such large-scale, thoughtful planning.

The master plan that evolved over the five-year DRI process called for creating a family-oriented "hometown" with a wide mix of residential units as well as office, industrial, and commercial uses. In 1979, just as a long recession began to abate, Broward County approved the plan. This slowdown and the long planning period provided significant benefits, allowing several factors to help Weston achieve the hometown goal. First, in the early 1980s as recovery came to south Florida, it was

RIGHT Waterways serve double duty as stormwater management areas and sites for homes.

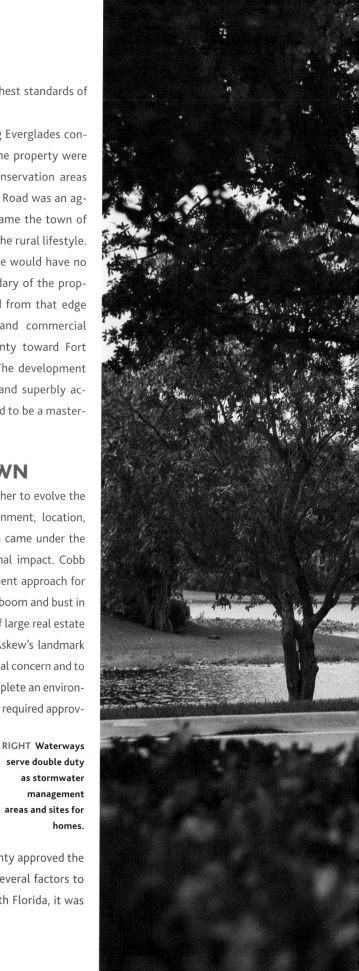

accompanied by a strong trend of northward population movement growing out of a relatively built-up Dade County into Broward County. The superior access to Weston that began to materialize as the freeways were completed opened the site to this primary housing market that was pushing northward.

Second, in 1980, the Florida legislature passed the Community Development District Act to help new communities pay for infrastructure. In 1981, Arvida formed the Indian Trace Community Development District, a pioneering effort to build water management, water and sewer systems, and roads in Weston. The Indian Trace district allowed infrastructure and community facilities to be built at lower costs than would be possible under ordinary financial methods, thereby providing more affordable housing sites for families. Over the years, the plan was reduced from more than 20,000 dwelling units to 17,000 to reflect market conditions and additional conservation areas.

OPPOSITE TOP A neighborhood school; Weston's Midtown Athletic Club; LEFT Peace Mound Archeological Park.

Cobb insisted that Arvida quality be incorporated throughout Weston, including the more affordable primary housing neighborhoods. So the plan for Weston, under the direction of Arvida's Roger Hall and Jim Motta, provided all neighborhoods with excellent infrastructure and well-landscaped roadways, waterways with riparian vegetation for habitat and aesthetic benefits, nearby schools, and parks. To make Weston a true town, the plan also created community-wide amenities that would be available to all residents. These amenities included numerous recreational facilities, locations for cultural or religious institutions, shopping, and jobs within the community. The plan emphasized the use of Arvida quality concepts to create a real hometown.

Plans for Weston designated major commercial and industrial development areas at the eastern edge of the site along I-75 and adjacent to Broward County's extensive existing development. Weston's residential areas would be buffered from this sprawl and the noise of freeway traffic by the commercial areas. These would be located near interchanges to the peripheral freeways, thus providing excellent access and protecting the residential neighborhoods from truck and commuter traffic.

The plans turned another necessary infrastructure feature into a major community amenity and organizing factor. An extensive series of new lakes and waterways were needed to provide stormwater runoff management as well as fill for the residential and commercial portions of the new town site. With proper planning, these waterways became the backbone of the residential neighborhoods in the site's interior, providing amenity and recreation as well as environmental benefit and wildlife habitat. And the western edge of the town nearest the Everglades would have wetland, agricultural, and conservation areas.

ELEMENTS OF THE WESTON PLAN

All the residential neighborhoods of Weston have a parklike setting that is created by the landscaped entries and roadways, local parks, underground utilities, and adjacent portions of Weston's 1,800 acres of waterways and riparian mitigation areas. Each neighborhood—ranging from moderately priced housing to country club mansions—has specific elements designated to create its own identity. Some focus on a school and park, others a large lake or golf course frontage. Windmill Ranches emphasizes its rural character and larger lots. Design controls provide for strict adherence to architectural and landscape guidelines and review of new or remodeled home developments. The community's covenants, codes, and restrictions require high levels of maintenance for the common roads, lakes, waterways, and landscape elements.

The Arvida team had an extensive marketing plan for the entire hometown, providing sales and visitor centers that stressed the overall assets of the new town and supported the builders of neighborhoods and commercial buildings. The use of sports events and club facilities for media coverage brought communication about Weston into local and target markets.

The major entry to the community was planned to be the I-75 interchange at Arvida Parkway. In a cooperative venture, Arvida and the Florida Department of Transportation planted 890 Royal Palms at the interchange, producing a skyline effect for travelers along the freeway and to residents returning home. Arvida also planted the median and sides of this road from the interchange to the main entrance. The road is now called Royal

Palm Boulevard in recognition of the extensive planting, and this prime access route remains a major community amenity and widely known Weston hallmark. Weston was also planned for complete systems of internal roadways serving each neighborhood or business district, sidewalks, bus shelters, and 46 miles of bike paths. Continuous street trees and landscape along major and minor roadways create linear greenways that constitute 60 miles of lush, well-maintained vegetation that is another hallmark of the city's appearance.

The plan has six elementary schools, each with its own five- to seven-acre park, two middle schools, and a high school, all on sites donated by Arvida. The community also has private schools and preschools. Recreational opportunities were meant to be available for all residents. The Weston Athletic Club has tennis, swimming, and fitness and spa facilities. The Weston Hills Country Club features two Robert Trent Jones, Jr., golf courses, tennis courts, and an aquatic facility. The community also has the Weston Tennis Center and the socially active Weston Community Center. Sites for a library and civic facilities were also set aside in the plan.

Weston's plan contains more than 320 acres of parks, including Peace Mound Park with a Tequesta Indian burial mound and a 102-acre regional park that has an Indian mound dating to the earliest settlements in the eastern Everglades (10,000 to 8,000 B.C.). More than 1,800 acres of protected open space are waterways, lakes, and riparian vegetation. The Indian Trace Development District, now a part of the city of Weston, has set aside 2,000 acres as wetland preserves at the western edge of the community.

Weston has 678 acres of planned business parks located on its eastern edge along I-75, including the 382-acre Weston Park of Commerce and the 240-acre Meridian Business Campus, whose tenants include a mix of Fortune 500 companies and local establishments. Weston has over 350 acres of community shopping centers and a town center. Centrally located, the town center was designed as a mixed-use center with a walkable main street district of retail, offices, and multifamily residential uses. Weston has five nationally recognized hotels and resorts.

LEFT Residential neighborhoods at Weston; **ABOVE** The Florida Cleveland Clinic.

Weston has some of its region's finest medical facilities. The Cleveland Clinic recognized Weston's central location and high standards of commercial development, and it located its first major Florida facility in the community. The facility is a fully integrated campus that includes a clinic with 150 physicians practicing 35 medical specialties and a full-service hospital with 150 beds. A nearby wellness center is located in West Palm Beach.

Finally, Weston was a leader in providing "soft infrastructure" and took Arvida's support of people-oriented activities into new territory. "Town Talk" was begun at Weston as an online interactive community to provide news of events, information on school and clubs, Community Center programs, and a bulletin board and forum on community issues. Town Talk continues to provide extensive programs at the Weston Community Center.

WESTON TODAY

In September 1996, residents in the Indian Trace Community Development District voted 90 percent in favor of incorporating Weston as a city. The entire master-planned community was included within the new municipal boundaries. The city of Weston later annexed the adjacent 1,300-acre, 6,388-unit Bonaventure Country Club community, on a site originally owned by Arvida and sold to be developed separately before Weston was planned. In that community, voters approved the annexation by a margin of two to one. The city of Weston later annexed lands to the west of U.S. 27, designating these as conservation areas and bringing its total area to more than 16,000 acres. By 2010, Weston was substantially built out as a community, and just over 100 acres of vacant developable remained from Arvida's original holdings.

In 2010, the population of the city was estimated to be 65,000. The 23,500 dwelling units are a mix of 78 percent single-family and 22 percent multifamily units. The median single-family home value in Weston was $470,000 in 2005, compared to $310,000 for Broward County. Median condominium value in 2005 was $230,000, compared to $187,000 for the county.

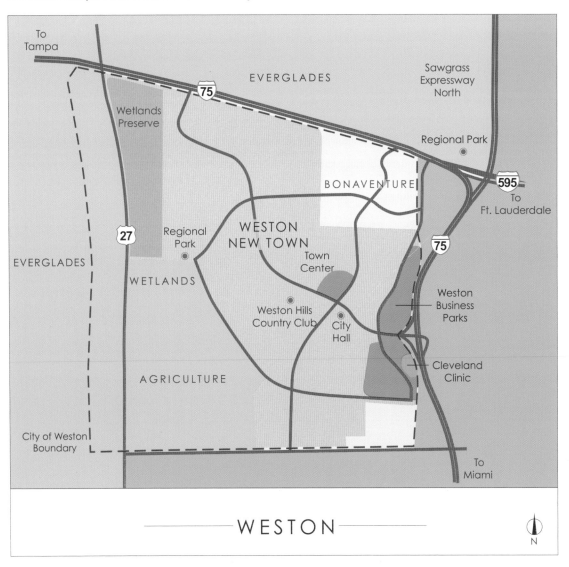

WESTON

Employment in Weston is estimated to be 25,000 to 30,000 jobs, a good jobs/housing balance within the town. Moreover, the employment consists mostly of well-paid jobs in offices, the Cleveland Clinic, and high-tech and service sectors that match well with the Weston labor force. However, even though Weston continues to be considered affordable, lower-paid employees have continuing difficulty finding affordable housing within the community.

The city has continued to use potable water and wastewater service from the nearby city of Sunrise that was originally contracted by Arvida, using the distribution system built by the Indian Trace Community Services District. The city also has continued the contracts that Arvida established for police, fire, and rescue services under contract with Broward County. These services are provided from three fire stations and one police station in the city. Weston currently has the lowest combined property taxes, municipal taxes, and fees in the county.

BELOW A street in Weston Town Center; OPPOSITE Office building in the town center.

The 2009 City of Weston Comprehensive Plan addresses smart growth by predicting, "As a planned community, with a defined footprint and density, the city will not contribute to the sprawl and continued expansion of utilities that has become a prominent development concern across the nation. The city is nearly built out, and as such, nearly all future projects will be redevelopment projects with existing infrastructure available."

Weston has won national recognition as a desirable community. It was rated by *Money* magazine in 2008 as the best place to live in the state of Florida, and the city with the largest job growth in the state from 2000 to 2005. *Business Week* ranked Weston as one of the "best affordable suburbs" in the United States in 2006.

Sawgrass

Jacksonville is a river city, situated on the wide and navigable St. Johns River in northeastern Florida. A commercial, industrial, and military city, the downtown is 16 miles from Jacksonville Beach, which developed over the years as an urban-oriented beach community, more similar to those up the southeast coast than to the beach-oriented communities of south Florida. Partly because of the cold winters that limited beach use, the long commute to the business center, and the transient nature of Jacksonville Beach, the city was not considered a suitable place for families to establish permanent residences. One lived up the river and went to the beach for summer fun.

Southeast of the large Jacksonville metropolitan area, which includes all of Duval County, is the more rural St. Johns County, between the St. Johns River and the Atlantic beaches, with historic St. Augustine at its center. A narrow panhandle of St. Johns County juts up along the Atlantic beaches into the Jacksonville metropolitan area. The town of Ponte Vedra Beach is at the north end of the panhandle, and the Ponte Vedra Country Club and Golf Course makes a distinct transition from south Jacksonville Beach to a less commercial, quieter, and higher-end residential character in St. Johns County.

RIGHT Homes on waterways; residential street with tree preservation; townhouses along golf and marsh areas; OPPOSITE The Tournament Players Clubhouse.

In this far southeast corner of the river city, directly south of Ponte Vedra Beach, James Stockton in 1972 began the development of 1,100-acre Sawgrass community. The son of one of the original 1930s developers of the Ponte Vedra Club, he was able to reroute a portion of Ponte Vedra Boulevard to increase the depth of the central beachfront at Sawgrass and began a beach community. In 1977, several factors came together that convinced Chuck Cobb to buy Sawgrass and transform it into an Arvida master-planned community.

THE "BUTLER" DID IT

The first factor was Chuck Cobb's and John Temple's interest in working in the north Florida market, having successfully established Arvida in south and central Florida. The opportunity arose to gain control of the small but well-begun Sawgrass property in the vicinity of Ponte Vedra Beach, which would fit well into the Arvida quality principles they had established as well as satisfy the long-term goals of James Stockton to expand his goals for the Ponte Vedra area. Under the direction of Peter Rummell, the development of an Arvida resort community began at Sawgrass.

Homes on a golf course, lakes, and marsh preserves at the Sawgrass Country Club.

The second and critically important factor was the solution of the historic difficulty of access from central Jacksonville to the beach. With only arterial roads traversing congested communities, the 16-mile journey to the beaches directly east of downtown was painful and inefficient. This poor access was to experience a sea change in a few years with the 1979 opening of J. Turner Butler Boulevard, a limited-access highway built by the Jacksonville Transportation Authority. This "road to nowhere," as the locals first called it, made a direct connection from I-95 in central Jacksonville to the beach. Running along undeveloped lands of Jacksonville's Southside, the limited-access expressway ended at Highway A1A at the border of south Jacksonville Beach and Ponte Vedra Beach. Downtown was now within an easy 20-minute commute to the beach and to Sawgrass. This route enabled the potential market for Sawgrass homes to include a wider mix of resort, recreation, and primary residential products ensuring a diverse community. And it became apparent that the "Butler"

in later years would open up the Southside to a new corridor of high-quality development for the metropolitan area. This prediction was borne out in a new campus of the University of North Florida, the development of the Mayo Clinic, and office campuses, business parks, and planned residential communities extending along Butler's perimeter.

GOLF AS A DESTINATION

An added attraction for Arvida was the potential to enhance a key ingredient for the area—well-developed golf courses. Although the Jacksonville climate limited beach use in the winter months, it was suitable for golf. The 1,100-acre Sawgrass Country Club had a fine 18-hole golf course, but marsh preservation issues allowed only a nine-hole addition to create a 27-hole course.

The lands to the west of Sawgrass extending to the Intracoastal Waterway were in large part controlled by the Fletchers, developers who in the mid-1970s had secured a 5,300-acre DRI approval from the state. They had started development and wanted to bring the Tournament Players Club (TPC) to their property but were having financial difficulties. Chuck Cobb saw the potential benefits in extending Sawgrass to the west and in bringing the TPC to the area.

In 1979, Arvida bought 1,300 acres of the Fletchers' land. In a bold attempt to put Sawgrass (and Jacksonville at the beach) on

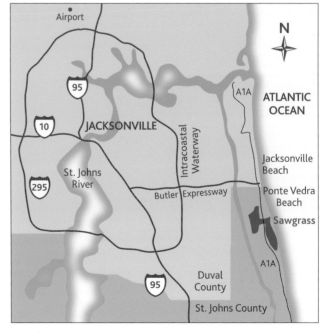

the map, Arvida gave 417 acres to the TPC at no cost for its first "stadium" golf course designed for television and spectators. The fiendishly difficult course designed by Pete and Alice Dye and its signature "Island Green"

hole are now renowned throughout the golfing world. The TPC relocated its headquarters from Washington, D.C., to Sawgrass in 1979. The TPC course and its televised and hugely attended tournaments put Jacksonville on the golfers' dream map.

Subsequently, another 18-hole course was added to the Players Club at Sawgrass for a total of 54 holes including the existing 18-hole Oak Bridge course, now called Ponte Vedra Country Club at Sawgrass. A Marriott Resort Hotel was added to the Players Club as well as golf villas. In the mid-1980s, Arvida considered adding 11,200 acres of the Fletchers' land to Sawgrass, but the Fletchers finally kept and developed it themselves as the

prestigious Marsh Landing Country Club with an 18-hole course designed by Ed Seay. To the south of the Players Club, the Plantation development added yet another course. With the original Ponte Vedra Country Club course and the Ponte Vedra Inn and Club, the St. Johns panhandle of the Jacksonville metropolitan area with 135 holes of high-quality golf and resort facilities had become a national destination and a great place to live.

SAWGRASS TODAY: A VITAL PART OF METROPOLITAN JACKSONVILLE

Jacksonville families continue to have summer or retirement homes at the beach but now consider Sawgrass Country Club and the Players Club at Sawgrass in the Ponte Vedra unincorporated area a good location for primary residences. In the 2000 census, Sawgrass itself had a permanent population of 5,000 with 1,500 families. Population should show substantial increases in the 2010 census as Sawgrass reaches buildout. Ponte Vedra now has an excellent school system. *Money* magazine named the area as the best place to live in Florida in 2005 and one of the 100 best places to live in the country.

The elements that make up the Sawgrass community include the 81 holes of golf and the three clubhouses: the Sawgrass Golf Club, the Tournament Players Club, and the Ponte Vedra Country Club at Sawgrass. For tennis, the Oak Bridge Tennis and Swim Center and the Sawgrass Racquet Club, named by *World Tennis Magazine* as one of America's top 50 tennis resorts, provide amenities. The Sawgrass Marriott hotel has a tennis facility, and nearby is the Association of Tennis Professionals National Headquarters.

The Sawgrass Beach Club is large and well equipped, serving all of Sawgrass and providing access to the extensive Atlantic beaches. Adjacent to the Beach Club are condominiums and villas for resort guests. The health and fitness club also serves all residents and guests. The 26-acre Sawgrass Village has 40 shops and restaurants on a lakefront setting, includes the 128-room Country Inn, and is host of the annual Fall Arts Festival.

ABOVE Parkway with golf-cart transportation; **OPPOSITE** The Tournament Players Club.

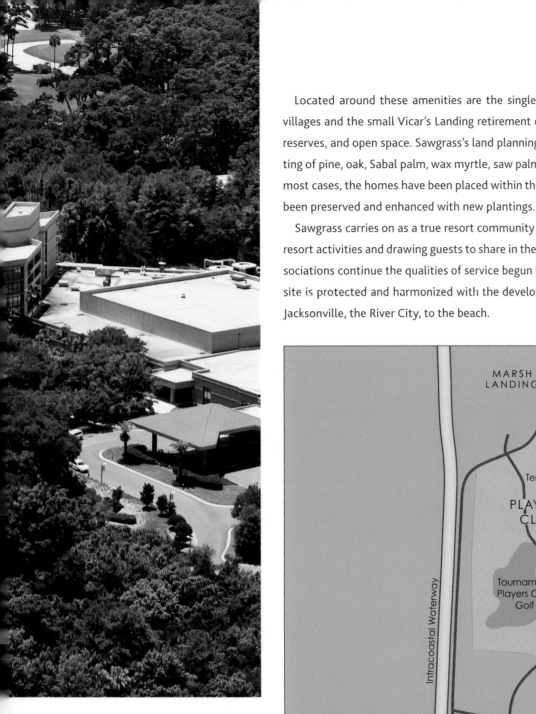

Located around these amenities are the single-family, patio-home, villa, townhouse, and condominium villages and the small Vicar's Landing retirement community set on extensive lakes and waterways, wildlife reserves, and open space. Sawgrass's land planning and architecture harmonize with the woodsy natural setting of pine, oak, Sabal palm, wax myrtle, saw palmetto trees, and other vegetation. In most cases, the homes have been placed within the natural setting, and tree cover has been preserved and enhanced with new plantings.

OPPOSITE The Sawgrass Marriott at the TPC; shops at Sawgrass Village.

Sawgrass carries on as a true resort community serving residents with a plethora of resort activities and drawing guests to share in their use. The clubs and community associations continue the qualities of service begun by Arvida. The natural beauty of the site is protected and harmonized with the development. In this way, Sawgrass played a key role in bringing Jacksonville, the River City, to the beach.

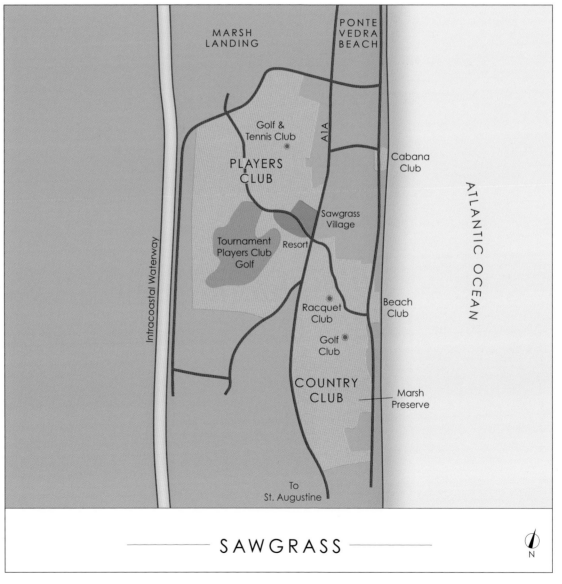

SAWGRASS

Willow Springs

ROSWELL, GEORGIA

Expanding into Georgia | **ARVIDA CORPORATION, 1978**

During the real estate recession of 1973 to 1975, Cobb and his team at Arvida were presented with many opportunities to expand into the Atlanta metropolitan area. The first acquisition, in 1975, was a 200-acre property known as Chimney Springs, located in the prestigious northeast suburbs. In 1978, Arvida gained control of 650 acres of rolling, heavily wooded land in the same general area as Chimney Springs. A local developer had just built a golf course and a few homes on a property that included the 27-acre Willow Lake, so Arvida named the community Willow Springs. The two projects gave Arvida a critical mass for marketing, development, and management purposes.

Arvida set out to make Willow Springs a country club community. It upgraded the 18-hole golf course and created a 13-court tennis center, began a 7,000-square-foot clubhouse, and set up the Willow Springs Country Club with a three-tier membership structure. The structure is one Arvida has used successfully in its other communities. It features a full golf and all other amenities tier at a higher price; a tennis, swim, fitness, and clubhouse intermediate tier; and a lower-priced social tier, including swim, fitness, and clubhouse use. Tennis and social members can get limited golf privileges for an extra fee.

LEFT Golf-frontage homes in the forest; OPPOSITE, TOP Championship golf; the Country Club of Roswell at Willow Springs.

Building and landscape controls were established, and local builders were selected to build the homes. Entry monuments and landscape at the entry and along the streets identified the new community. A 12-acre neighborhood shopping center was built at the entry to the community. Wherever possible, the tree cover was preserved and structures were designed to blend into the attractive natural environment. The Willow Springs Homeowners Association was organized to manage and maintain the common areas.

Using its now well-developed strategy of a stable of local builders operating under tight design controls and a unified community image, Arvida was able to accelerate the buildout, and by 1984 all of the 683 single-family homes were sold. A private equity club was set up, and Arvida sold the golf and social club to the 366 members. Because the community was located within the well-known and upscale city of Roswell, the new private club changed its name to the Country Club of Roswell.

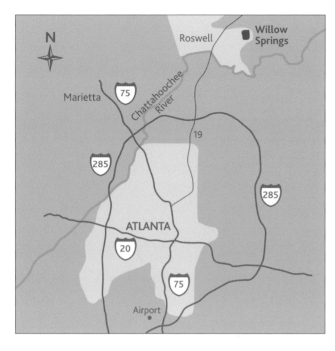

Today, the community is known as both the Country Club of Roswell and Willow Springs. Perception in the real estate marketplace is that the Willow Springs and Arvida names have a great reputation among knowledgeable Atlanta homebuyers. The Willow Springs Homeowners Association continues to maintain the high standards of community development set by Arvida. To the Atlanta area golfing set, the Roswell name brings regional location and prestige together.

The Country Club of Roswell has been identified with social events such as weddings and charitable golf tournaments. Roswell, a city of 90,000, has a town center, shopping centers, civic facilities, and excellent parks along the Chattahoochee River. The city has 40,000 jobs, with a favorable jobs/housing balance. Employers include the regional headquarters campus of Kimberly Clark close to Willow Springs. The area has good schools and public services. By having both prestige and nearby employment centers, the community benefits and is known as a sanctuary from the hustle and bustle of metropolitan Atlanta.

As a primary home, suburban country club, family-oriented neighborhood, Willow Springs was and continues to be a favored place in the Atlanta region. Arvida still is remembered as creating a lasting community with high development standards and an innovative club structure.

LEFT Homes at Willow Springs; BELOW The aquatic center and shopping area of Willow Springs; OPPOSITE Homes with golf and lakeside amenities.

Cocoplum

CORAL GABLES, FLORIDA
Completing "The City Beautiful" | **ARVIDA CORPORATION, 1979**

In 1979, Cobb and Temple gained control of a 350-acre tract of land along the shores of Biscayne Bay in Coral Gables, Florida. It was the largest undeveloped waterfront parcel close to Miami and bordered the city's historic and beautiful Coconut Grove section. It also was one of the last large, developable parcels in the planned community of Coral Gables, known as "The City Beautiful."

Coral Gables had earned the motto. First planned in the 1920s by George Merrick, the city had gone through the ups and downs of the Great Depression, hurricanes, and World War II to emerge as one of the most beautiful and successful planned communities of the 20th century in America. A product of the then waning City Beautiful movement, it was also influenced by the European Garden City movement and the garden suburbs such as Riverside, Illinois, pioneered by Frederick Law Olmsted.

Between 1921 and 1926, George Merrick acquired and led the planning and development of a good portion of the city that exists today. He relied on landscape architect Frank Button to produce a complete master plan for the roadways, waterways, and residential and commercial elements of the city and artist Denman Fink to design the many entrances, gates, plazas, circles, promenades, and fountains that gave the city its clear identity.

Like Olmsted, Button and Fink understood the key to this new suburban city was the design of the roads as public gardens. They wanted to make the roads a place for people not just cars—real "parkways." The

LEFT View from Cocoplum along Biscayne Bay to downtown Miami; **RIGHT** A typical residence; sports at the Cocoplum Club.

parkways of Coral Gables are what clearly distinguish it whenever one enters the city through its memorable gateways. The generous rights-of-way included broad, landscaped shoulders with only enough paving to move vehicles. The tropical climate required shade to enable people to move about comfortably, so every

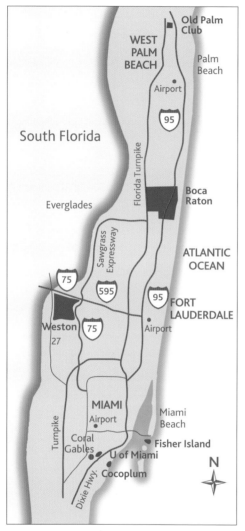

roadway in the city was planted with various tropical trees, creating a dense arbor of shade throughout. The trees in the residential districts were planted in generous curb-free city-maintained planting strips using tough St. Augustine grasses that could tolerate the shade, absorb the torrential rains, and easily accommodate parking or service vehicles. Where present, sidewalks are at the edge of the rights-of-way next to the residential lots. Homes are set back, with open, unfenced front yards. The overall effect, continuing to this day, is a hospitable, neighborly, and pedestrian-friendly environment, a true "public garden" throughout the city.

COCOPLUM IN CORAL GABLES

Besides the public garden character and strict zoning and architectural controls of Coral Gables, two other major elements of the historic city plan were relevant to the planning of the Cocoplum site. First, Merrick's plan featured major waterways that traversed the entire city and connected it to Biscayne Bay, all accessible by small boat. The largest, the Coral Gables Waterway, emptied into the bay at the Cocoplum site. Early plans called for a yacht basin to be built on the waterway near Cocoplum Circle where the major north-south routes of the city crossed the waterway. In their plans, Merrick and Button envisioned a series of islands and waterways running south from Cocoplum Circle down the long Biscayne Bay coast of Coral Gables.

Second, the coastline of the southern section of Coral Gables was edged by mangrove hammocks with several small horseshoe-shaped coves that had sandy beaches on Biscayne Bay. One of these was Tahiti Beach at Cocoplum. In the 1920s, when Merrick built the Biltmore Hotel, he used Venetian gondolas to ferry guests four miles from the hotel grounds down the waterway to Tahiti Beach, expanded for the hotel by extensive clearing of the mangroves along the bay shore.

Arvida was able to implement the yacht basin, island, and waterway concepts of Merrick's plan. However, in the more than 50 years since the original development, Tahiti Beach has been returned to its small horseshoe shape by natural processes, and the mangroves have reclaimed the bay shore. The plan would preserve all of the areas within Cocoplum that contained those mangroves. Over time, the largest portion of southern Coral Gables along the Biscayne Bay shore would become mangrove preserves and parks like Matheson Hammock County Park, on a

A street in Cocoplum.

large tract of public land farther south in the city. Cocoplum was to be one of the last of the island-and-waterway concepts of the historic plan.

THE ISLANDS OF COCOPLUM MASTER PLAN

The plan for the 350-acre Islands of Cocoplum that was prepared by SWA Group was approved by the city in 1979. It included 286 home sites on four islands connected by bridges; a 180-slip private yacht club and marina directly connected to the Coral Gables Waterway; 80 acres of mangrove preserves; a recreation clubhouse, a pool, and basketball and tennis courts. Following the Coral Gables precedent, an elaborate entry gateway and landscaped median and arbor mark the road leading in from Cocoplum Circle with entry monuments, fully landscaped roadways, traffic circles, and residential commons. The custom homes were built under strict city codes and Arvida's design review.

SWA Group's original plan envisioned nominal one-half-acre residential lots for three of the four islands. The fourth island directly on Biscayne Bay (which included Tahiti Beach) was proposed to have 80 clustered patio homes for maintenance-free living and extensive open space and waterfront access ways. When the city turned down this concept, Arvida then proposed a large-lot, high-end community with a separate security gate for this Tahiti Beach island. This approach was approved by Coral Gables, and this fourth island of Cocoplum became a successful community within a community.

LEFT Custom homes on common greens at Cocoplum; **ABOVE** The Tahiti Beach island faces on Biscayne Bay.

The environmental regulations of the 1970s and 1980s began to recognize the critical importance of the mangroves for shoreline and habitat protection. Big storm surges and hurricane devastation also generated popular support for mangrove protection on the bayfront. The Cocoplum plan preserved the existing mangroves, and the internal waterways between the islands were heavily vegetated where there were no mangroves. The plan also retained the small horseshoe beach with its moving sand profiles. In the few circumstances where the mangroves had not reestablished along the bayfront, seawalls would have to provide limited protection.

COCOPLUM AND SMART GROWTH

Arvida created Cocoplum as a new waterfront neighborhood, building on the traditions and historic plans set 50 years before its development. The Islands of Cocoplum respected and carefully implemented key provisions of the historic overall city plan, while addressing modern understanding of environmental and sustainable development issues such as mangrove preservation. In these ways, Cocoplum is a fine example of master-planned community implementation over time.

BELOW Continuing the Coral Gables parkways and circles into Cocoplum; OPPOSITE, TOP The Islands of Cocoplum, yacht harbor, and mangrove preserves; OPPOSITE, BOTTOM Boats along the Cocoplum waterways.

In terms of smart growth principles, Cocoplum was an infill site in a well-planned and growth-controlled city. It was bordered by luxury single-family developments to the immediate south, west, and north. The city plan, codes, and surrounding neighborhoods favored similar development on the remaining Cocoplum site. In itself, Cocoplum did not have a mix of land uses, a wide range of housing types, or a variety of transportation opportunities, although it had excellent access to the convergence of the city's main arterial network. It was a very distinctive community with a strong sense of place, critical environmental areas were preserved, and stakeholder participation and fair and predictable development decisions prevailed. Planned growth for Coral Gables contributed to the city's residential, recreational, and environmental assets.

Coto de Caza

ORANGE COUNTY, CALIFORNIA
Bringing Arvida quality to California | ARVIDA CORPORATION, 1982

As part of Arvida's effort to diversify outside of Florida and Georgia, Chuck Cobb, John Temple, and their team entered the southern California market in the early 1980s. They acquired control from one of Penn Central's other subsidiaries of the 5,000-acre Coto de Caza, one of Orange County's oldest entitled planned communities, which was still largely undeveloped. SWA Group provided advice on the design approach to this beautiful secluded valley, and in 1983 a revised master plan was prepared locally and approved for 5,000 homes; enhanced access; new golf, tennis, and additional equestrian amenities; and increased landscaping and design controls catering to the high end of the residential market. Similar to the Arvida approach in Florida, a program of premier club and sports activities was undertaken, such as the 1984 Olympic competitions held at the Equestrian Center, the development of the Vic Braden Tennis College, and two Robert Trent Jones, Jr., golf courses.

RIGHT **A cluster of estates at Coto de Caza;** BELOW **The Coto de Caza Spa and Sports Center.**

Coto de Caza means "hunting preserve" in Portuguese, and the original plan in 1964 was for a hunting and equestrian community, carrying on the tradition of the valley. It is an unincorporated area of Orange County and encompasses a long, narrow, and naturally beautiful north-south valley with heavy riparian vegetation in the central arroyo and extending partway up the surrounding hillsides. The community is bounded by open space and preserves, including O'Neill Regional Park, Thomas F. Riley Wilderness Park, the National Audubon Society's Starr Ranch Sanctuary, and Ronald W. Caspers Wilderness Park. Interstate 5, which links Los Angeles to San Diego, is five miles to the west. Access from northern Orange County is by the Foothill Transportation Corridor.

The golf course
in the valley.

THE PLAN

The Arvida plan retained the equestrian facilities but by adding tennis, golf, and club activities turned Coto de Caza into one of the largest and most desirable private gated communities in California. Development of the

new plan began in 1986 with larger lots on the surrounding hills, which had sweeping views of the golf courses running down the center of the valley, along with clusters of homes below on the ranchland knolls and side hills in the valley. Today, the community is built out with approximately 18,000 residents, served by a private golf and racquet club, a tennis center, and a spa and sports club. Other recreational features include the Coto Valley Equestrian Center, site of the 1984 Olympic equestrian competitions, 40 miles of equestrian trails, and the Orange County Polo Club. A small community park has picnic areas and playing fields. The other nonresidential uses are the Coto Valley Country Club, the Coto de Caza

General Store, and the Lodge at Coto de Caza. To retain the privacy of the community, no schools are located within the gates. The remainder of the community comprises hillside estates and clusters of homes surrounded by open space, golf courses, and natural riparian vegetation areas. The community has three homeowners associations: CZ Master Association, Coto de Caza (The Village), and Los Ranchos Estates.

Outside the south gates, the Thomas F. Riley Wilderness Park was given to Orange County by the community. This park contains 475 acres of extensive sycamore and oak groves and heritage trees. It has six miles of hiking, mountain bike, and equestrian trails and a nature center. Directly adjacent to Riley Park is the Wagon Wheel School and Sports Park serving Coto de Caza and the surrounding communities. Schools, shopping, religious, commercial, employment, and civic facilities are located outside the gates in the nearby city of Rancho Santa Margarita and the communities of Mission Viejo, Lake Forest, and Irvine.

A PRIVATE ENCLAVE

Coto de Caza is a highly amenitized private residential enclave with home prices starting at $1 million and going far beyond that. It is a specialized community and is extremely successful in accomplishing its limited goals. It is less of a complete community than many other examples in this book and more a series of well-planned private neighborhoods. The elements of the site—secluded location, private security, natural beauty, and surrounding open space—are enhanced by an abundance of clubs, sports facilities, and amenities, creating a highly valued community.

In Chuck Cobb's words, "I have followed the development of Coto since its first year of development in 1964 by Macco Development, who was our partner at Rancho California and with whom we shared personnel. I always believed the Arvida team could make Coto a better community and I am pleased we accomplished that objective in the 1980s."

Looking east to the Audubon sanctuary and Caspers Wilderness Park.

COBB'S MASTER-PLANNED COMMUNITIES

The Walt Disney World

Resort

In 1984, after a merger between Arvida and the Walt Disney Company, Chuck Cobb joined Disney's board of directors and became chairman and CEO for Disney Development Company, which was charged with managing and developing all of Disney's real estate assets. His first major task was a master plan for the 28,000-acre Disney World near Orlando. The previous plan for Disney World was to create an entertainment and vacation resort that would be home to multiple attractions and resort accommodations and where visitation would go beyond a day trip to the Magic Kingdom. A strong start was made on this plan, but by 1984 this overall goal was yet to be achieved.

Opened in 1971, Disney World had developed the Magic Kingdom and in 1982 added the Epcot (the "Experimental Prototype Community of Tomorrow") theme park. Disney had developed 5,000 hotel rooms at Disney World while an array of established hotel brands had developed 50,000 rooms in the nearby Orlando area. Disney Development was charged with further

LEFT The Caribbean Beach—one of the Vacation Clubs; **BELOW** Monorail connecting Epcot to the Magic Kingdom; the Grand Floridian hotel at the Magic Kingdom.

shaping the world-class attractions (the Magic Kingdom is the number-one theme park in the world with over 17 million annual visits) and the existing and additional resort functions into a true overall resort experience and by doing so, increase the company's economic yields from these properties. For example, Disney Development projected a market for 50,000 additional hotel rooms on the Disney World site when only 5,000 existed in 1984.

Cobb formed a team of Arvida and Disney executives that included Peter Rummell and Roger Hall, each with extensive experience in resort development at Arvida, and Wing Chao from Disney's in-house staff, who had considerable experience in planning and building Disney attractions and facilities. Cobb also called upon the SWA Group and economic, engineering, and other consultants with resort and recreation experience to assist in preparing a strategic master plan for Disney World.

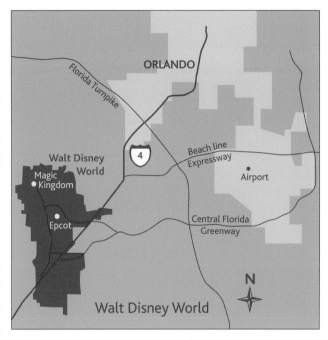

A MASTER PLAN FOR DISNEY WORLD

The original 1967 approvals for Disney World involved a special district set up by the state of Florida, the Reedy Creek Improvement District (RCID). The RCID and its Comprehensive General Plan had almost the same status under Florida state law as a city or county had in regulating development. The new master plan was intended as a strategic document for Disney Development Company, and it was thought that as new strategic policies were established through this plan, the official RCID plan would be modified as required by law.

Cobb's team carried the land analysis in the RCID plan further by using the then new Landsat satellite to identify areas suitable for future development based on soil types and capacities, depth of muck, drainage, depth to water table, and vegetation. Engineering consultants added water management, utilities, and transportation components, including roads, bus, monorail, and water travel modes. Economic consultants provided projections of market trends nationally and in the Orlando recreation complex, and the Disney members of the planning team dealt with visitation issues, and projections and opportunities for new venues, accommodations, and needed support facilities and infrastructure.

LEFT The new resort area adjacent to Epcot, accessible by boat or bus and on foot.

The challenge for the new management team headed by Cobb was to better use and build upon the incredible entertainment resources and investments represented by the Magic Kingdom and Epcot. The newly opened Epcot had cost over $1 billion but was isolated from tourist accommodations and not attracting enough visitors. The plan needed to consider what new attractions or uses would add to the resort experience

and improve visitation. Also, the locations of the themed attractions, visitor entries, transportation corridors, and accommodations needed to be better connected and coordinated in a way that made moving around the property less time consuming and stressful for guests.

No one in the world manages a controlled environment better than Disney inside its great attractions, but that level of quality and entertainment needed to be expanded to the other parts of the resort outside the attractions. A small beginning had been made in 1971 at the Contemporary and Polynesian hotels on the lakes next to the Magic Kingdom. Water transportation to the Magic Kingdom and the hotels from large parking areas created a unique and fun way to arrive and move about. The Contemporary had the monorail whisking through the lobby, and the Polynesian was served by the monorail and ferry. These themed hotels with their landscaped grounds and facilities along with the monorail and lake transport brought the theme park experience into the visitor accommodations. Unfortunately, after 1971 Disney had not followed up on more of these well-received visitor accommodations.

THE RESORT OF THE FUTURE

Cobb's team prepared a master plan that identified prime development sites, open space, environmental areas, and resort and transportation concepts for the entire property. It identified sites for future attractions, amenities, varied visitor accommodations, and a large planned community located south of I-4 that later became Celebration. Another bold proposal was to expand the idea of Epcot by including state-of-the-art high-tech education, research campuses, and business parks for next-generation global companies, with a worldwide conference center and shopping and entertainment complexes.

To expand the resort experience at this new Disney development, the Cobb plan proposed that a significant number of new Disney-themed hotels and other accommodations be built in areas directly adjacent to Epcot, the Magic Kingdom, and the newly designated attractions in the plan. The standard corporate-branded hotels at Lake Buena Vista were not adding to the Disney experience and did not include a variety of recreation ex-

LEFT The Michael Graves–designed Dolphin Hotel; **RIGHT** Disney's BoardWalk Inn.

periences that could be unique to Disney. These proposed accommodations could be hotels, timeshares, and a new "vacation club" experience in walkable, environmentally based villages.

Another major proposal involved how people moved around Walt Disney World. The monorail was an enchanting mover of people between the two attractions and was unique to Disney in the United States. It was a great image-maker but was not effective in moving the large volumes of people necessary. And even with Disney-scale budgets, extending the monorail to the Lake Buena Vista hotels was prohibitively expensive. The use of water transportation, begun earlier at the Magic Kingdom, was very successful in moving large numbers of people and was an entertaining experience in itself. Therefore, the plan proposed that the new themed accommodations should be served by waterways and boat transportation systems connecting directly to the attractions, as well as by the roadway systems.

Disney formed a "Futures Conference" to hear ideas about the future from visionaries such as James Rouse, chairman of the Enterprise Foundation; Robert Lucky, executive director of Bell Labs; John Naisbitt, of the Naisbitt

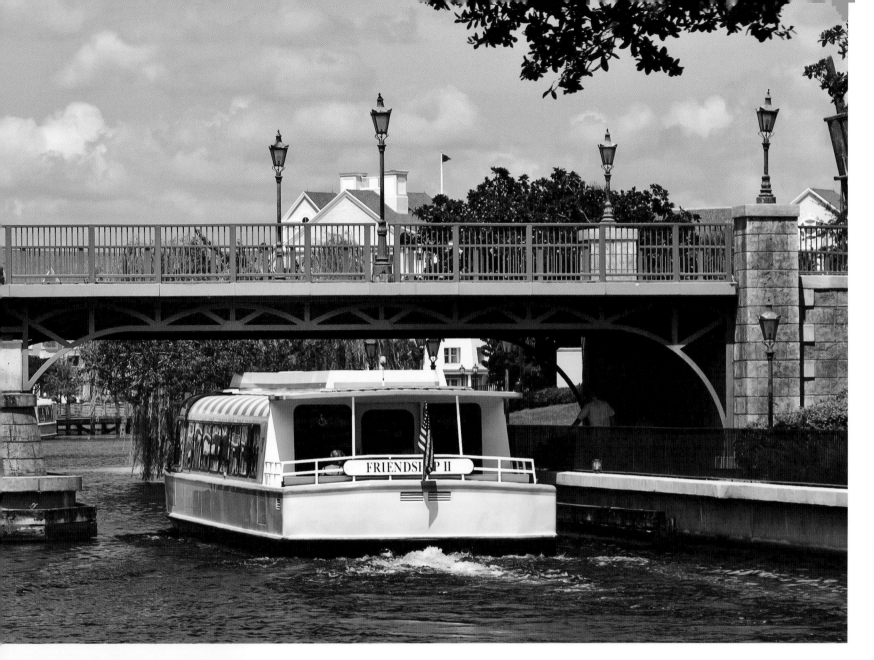

Group; and architects Jaquelin Robertson and Michael Graves. They were asked to assess the concepts of the master plan created by the SWA Group, Cobb, and the Disney development team and how these plans related to their ideas of the future. The Futures Conference participants supported the major concepts to create a complete resort experience with "entertainment, environment, and architecture" in accord with the larger role they believed such entertainment activities would play in the future of families and society. The new themed accommodations and the expansion of the special modes of transportation such as the waterways around the resort and the new attractions also gained their enthusiastic support. They supported a proposed technology, research, and business center, but Michael Eisner and other Disney executives voiced concern over potential effects on the entertainment areas.

Consensus also favored the idea that the major planned community situated away from the resort should be on property separated by environmental preserves and located across I-4. This area later was to become, under

ABOVE Cruising from Epcot to the yacht club, beach club, and BoardWalk lake; LEFT Walking from Epcot to the resort accommodations.

Disney Development, the town of Celebration. After the conference, the Cobb plan was put into effect and would set the future of Walt Disney World over the next few decades.

On May 9, 1986, the Urban Land Institute celebrated its 50th anniversary at Walt Disney World. Chuck Cobb presented the new Walt Disney World Master Plan to approximately 5,000 people. The Disney presentation of the combined entertainment and real estate approach was well received.

BUILDING THE WALT DISNEY WORLD RESORT

Chuck Cobb's team and Disney Development began to sketch out a phased roadmap of essential steps to fulfill the goal of making the property into a multiple entertainment activity and destination resort: the Walt Disney

World Resort. Experience showed that the most successful resorts create, control, and deliver a highly amenitized environment to the guests from the moment they arrive on the property until the moment they depart. This achievement became the overriding goal.

The plan proposed the use of a total "entertainment environment" for the entire property. This began with "entertainment architecture" to create hotels and other real estate products like golf villas, condominium villages, and timeshares in the right locations as designated in the plan. Disney accommodations would become an integral part of the resort experience.

Connections between the various components of the resort received special landscape, streetscape, and signage treatments to create a seamless resort environment. More efficient use of the existing monorail, without any costly expansion, and more waterway and boat transportation would be a cost-effective way to enhance the entertainment value of transportation around the resort. An expanded variety of visitor accommodations, including vacation ownership, was developed and marketed under the Disney brand, bringing in new markets and increased revenue sources. Cobb's idea for Disney Development Company to blend Disney's outstanding entertainment capabilities with Arvida's resort operations and real estate know-how to create the Walt Disney World Resort had begun.

The first phases of the master plan were quickly set into motion by Disney Development working closely with Disney Imagineering. First priority was to add the new resort accommodations in the area next to the Magic Kingdom around the Seven

ABOVE The Wilderness Lodge at the Magic Kingdom; RIGHT The Caribbean Beach Club in the foreground with Epcot beyond.

Seas Lagoon and Bay Lake, adjacent to the Contemporary and Polynesian hotels. These new hotels became the Grand Floridian and the Wilderness Lodge; later, the adjacent Wilderness Villas were added. The existing Palm and Magnolia golf courses to the west of the Magic Kingdom broadened the resort experience, and a village of timeshare accommodations would be added to the golf resort and its extensive club facilities. The Magic Kingdom area in this way was transformed into a multiple-function resort destination.

The next priority was an ambitious expanded destination resort area directly adjacent to Epcot. It would include new Disney hotels close enough to walk or take a tram or boat to Epcot. The Tishman organization had previously signed an agreement to build two new hotels at Lake Buena Vista on the far eastern side of Walt Disney World. The challenge for Disney Development was to convince the Tishman organization to build these two hotels not at Lake Buena Vista but instead in the Epcot area and to hire Michael Graves as the architect. The Tishman organization was very reluctant to move its two hotels; however, after many meetings, most of which were orchestrated by Michael Eisner, Disney Development convinced Tishman to go forward with the Dolphin and Swan hotels, dramatically adding to the next phase of Disney Development's plan.

The next challenge was the location for Eisner's idea of a Hollywood studio tour. Again the proposed lake and waterway system adjacent to Epcot was selected by Disney Development and implemented by the design team. The World Showcase Lagoon in the center of Epcot would be connected to a landscaped waterway and series of lakes running through the resort accommodations. Sleek, low-slung riverboats similar to those in Paris or Amsterdam could take visitors directly from Epcot to the Boardwalk, the Yacht Club, the Beach Club, the iconic 1,500-room Dolphin Hotel, the 750-room Swan Hotel, and the Hollywood studio tour.

The vacation clubs concept, where one could own a timeshare or fractional interest under Disney management and on the Walt Disney World property, was then carried out with great success in the Caribbean Beach Resort, Port Orleans, and Old Key West themed villages located adjacent to the attractions. Downtown Disney provided new energy, shopping, and entertainment at Lake Buena Vista, bringing that area's amenities into line with the new resort areas. The choices of resort activities and accommodations were broadened significantly by the plan, and each area of Walt Disney World had a special and fun identity that contributed to the overall resort feeling.

ANAHEIM, PARIS, AND AFTER

During Cobb's leadership, a new plan was begun for Disneyland at Anaheim, California. It was carried forth in the 1990s to become the Anaheim/Disneyland Resort Plan by SWA Group working with the city of Anaheim, Disney Development, and Walt Disney Imagineering. These efforts again stressed creating an overall resort on the 1,100-acre Anaheim property. Significantly, the plans included a comprehensive program by Disney and the city to increase the quality of the public and private developments surrounding the property, thus incorporating those areas for the first time into the world-renowned Disneyland resort environment.

RIGHT Active vacationers at the Caribbean Beach Club; **OPPOSITE** A boat at the BoardWalk.

Cobb also led the successful effort to acquire a site for Euro Disney in Marne-la-Vallée, outside of Paris. Before Cobb's arrival and the formation of Disney Development, the previous management team was convinced that Disney's first international resort and entertainment center should be in Spain. Florida and Spain have certain physical similarities, and Disney executives wanted to repeat their Florida success in Spain. For several years, Disney executives had visited sites near Barcelona and other coastal towns.

Cobb joined Disney four months before Michael Eisner and Frank Wells had become CEO and chief operating officer, respectively, of Disney. During that time, Cobb had discovered the 4,000-acre Marne-la-Vallée site with its rapid-rail line into Paris and adjacent expressway connecting to other major European cities. The best part was the French government was prepared to sell the site to Disney for agricultural land prices of a few hundred dollars an acre. In the 1950s, President Charles de Gaulle selected several sites near Paris for future community development and froze the zoning and land prices. Marne-la-Vallée was one of those sites. It was a great opportunity that Eisner and Wells welcomed despite the view of many former Disney executives that the company should go to Spain. Development quickly ensued on this new European venture.

In 1987, just at the time that Disney chose to sell Arvida to JMB Realty, Chuck Cobb was asked by President Ronald Reagan and Vice President George H. W. Bush to serve as an assistant and then undersecretary of commerce. He left the field of community development to begin five years of public service in the Department of Commerce and as a U.S ambassador.

Peter Rummell, a key Arvida executive, was named president of Disney Development by Cobb and in the following years successfully carried out many of the plans initiated during Cobb's tenure. When Disney Development was merged into Disney Imagineering, Rummell led that group in building 20,000 resort accommodations near Epcot and the Magic Kingdom and expanded on the concepts of Disney resorts throughout the world.

Cullasaja Country Club

As CEO of Arvida Disney, in the mid-1980s Chuck Cobb expanded the geographic reach of Arvida planned communities to the scenic Blue Ridge Mountains in the far southwest corner of North Carolina. The 685-acre Cullasaja property was situated in the Nantahala National Forest at 4,250 feet above sea level and a 2½-hour drive from the Atlanta metropolitan area. This region's natural setting and cool mountain air during the summer were enhanced by the golf traditions begun by Bobby Jones in the 1930s with the establishment of the nearby Highlands Country Club and other fine golf facilities.

The Arvida plan established an 18-hole Arnold Palmer golf course and driving range, a clubhouse, and a six-court tennis center. Underground utilities, a security gate, and 281 single-family homes were planned in this

recreational community. The homes were carefully sited to preserve the forest cover. Design regulations and community covenants controlled the design, construction, and maintenance of all buildings and structures.

Lake Ravenel is located within the community and offers canoeing, kayaking, and bass fishing. The Cullasaja River and its tributaries, waterfalls, and hiking trails meander throughout the heavily forested property.

Today, Cullasaja Country Club is fully built out as a private club community. Arvida sold the club in 2000 to 297 members, and the club has established a membership-by-invitation limit of 330 members. The club has added a state-of-the art fitness center open all year long.

The residents of Cullasaja are mostly seasonal and use the town of Highlands, North

Carolina, 4.5 miles away on Highway 64, for shopping and other services. Highlands has a permanent population of 3,200, expanding to about 18,000 in the summer. Also nearby on Highway 64 is the town of Cashiers. Asheville, the closest major city, is 1½ hours away.

The club-based recreational community with its natural beauty, mountain views, and salubrious climate make Cullasaja attractive to second-home buyers. Its most important smart growth accomplishment is the careful way the development harmonizes with the natural resources of these National Forest lands and meets the multiple-use goals of the U.S. Forest Service in a very practical and sustainable way.

OPPOSITE Homes along the golf course and lake; LEFT The Clubhouse at Cullasaja; the golf course and homes in the forest; ABOVE The Cullasaja community overlooking the lake in fall color.

The use of National Forest land for private clubs and gated communities provides the benefit of private funds to maintain the quality of the forest environment. Benefits also flow to local communities in the form of jobs and an economic base for the permanent population. What is less evident without more local knowledge of the region is whether the benefits balance the loss of public access to these lands. With golf development of this area dating back 80 years, the assumption would be that the high quality that Arvida added to the region with Cullasaja maintained or enhanced a positive balance of public benefit.

Fisher Island with South Miami Beach in the background; ABOVE The pool at the beach club; the Vanderbilt Mansion, part of the Fisher Island Club; OPPOSITE Condominiums along the bay.

Fisher Island

In 1992 Chuck Cobb became chairman of the board of Fisher Island, a premier real estate development on a 216-acre island in the city of Miami Beach. The Mutual Benefit Life Insurance Company had begun a development in the 1980s but had difficulty with its implementation. Cobb brought his experience in high-end resort clubs and residential communities and was able to increase sales of the luxury condominiums, leading to the successful accomplishment of the development plan.

A PRIVATE ISLAND

The island bore the name of Miami Beach–founder Carl Fisher and was once part of the Miami Beach peninsula. In 1905, the 216-acre island was separated from the rest of Miami Beach by the dredging of a shipping channel, which provided direct access from the Atlantic Ocean to the Port of Miami on Biscayne Bay. According to legend, Fisher traded the island to William Vanderbilt in exchange for Vanderbilt's famous yacht,

The yacht harbor and condominiums.

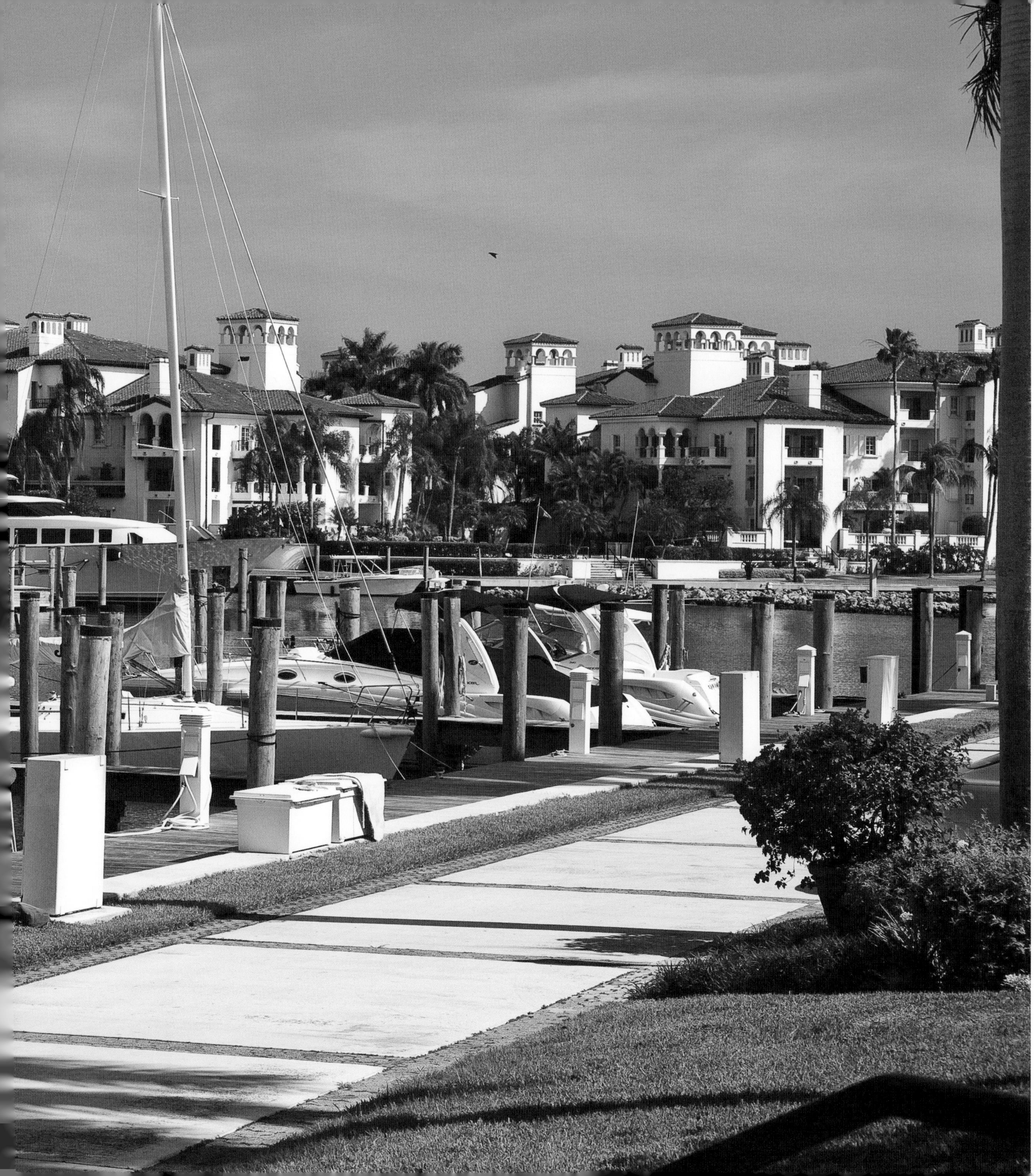

the *Eagle*. Beginning in 1925, Vanderbilt developed a magnificent retreat on the island with a Mediterranean-style mansion on the beach, lush landscaping, guest houses, tennis courts, swimming pools, and a nine-hole golf course. After a long period of different wealthy owners, a development plan was established that would turn Vanderbilt's grand private island into a world-class residential community and exclusive club.

Accessible only by a private auto ferry, boat, or helicopter, the island has 750 luxury, Mediterranean-style condominiums and an equal number of equity club members. In 2010, prices for the condominiums ranged from $500,000 to $17 million, with club entry and dues correspondingly high.

RAISING EQUITY AND PRESTIGE

Cobb brought in Frank Weed, former vice president of Arvida for Boca West, and they converted all the recreational facilities into a private equity club in which the homeowners own all the recreational amenities. This

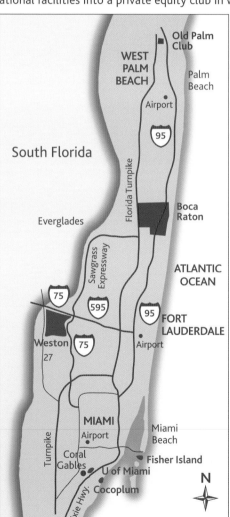

step was necessary to raise the capital to defray the high infrastructure costs and high levels of maintenance required to develop the self-contained island. It also set the world-class standard for the community. Club-owned amenities included the Beach Club and private beach, the restored and renovated Vanderbilt mansion as the main clubhouse, circa 1925 cottages and guest suites, the renovated P.B. Dye nine-hole golf course, three outdoor and one indoor swimming pools, two deepwater marinas with 118 slips, the 18-court Racquet Club, the 22,000-square-foot Spa Internazionale, and party and commercial facilities.

The island has a private elementary school as well as a fire station and post office. A private ferry service for automobiles and passengers is available at the nearby MacArthur Causeway between Downtown Miami and South Miami Beach for the ten-minute trip to the island.

The 48-unit Fisher Island Hotel and Resort was awarded Zagat's "best hotel in Miami" designation. Guests have access to the recreational facilities, ferry service, golf-cart rentals, the spa, the beach, and excellent restaurants. The hotel features a members-only private island vacation experience.

In 2011, Fisher Island has been mostly built out and enjoys the high standard of maintenance expected for a private club community. With fewer than 2,000 residents and guests, the 216-acre island and its elaborate amenities establish a level of quality and expense that is not reproducible in many locations around the world. In his two-year tenure as chairman of the development group, Cobb demonstrated that developing a private equity club to create both exclusiveness and an entitled sense of place could allow the development to succeed.

RIGHT Golf-frontage condominiums; ABOVE A mix of housing types.

Kirkwood

Mountain Resort

KIRKWOOD, CALIFORNIA
Year-round resort in the Lake Tahoe region | COBB PARTNERS, 1994

Kirkwood Mountain Resort is about 30 miles south of Lake Tahoe and 177 miles from the San Francisco Bay area on California State Highway 88. The access from Highway 88, rather than the traffic-choked I-80 or Highway 50, gives Kirkwood a several-hour travel advantage over other Lake Tahoe skiing areas. Kirkwood is an exclusive family resort conveniently accessible to the major population centers of the San Francisco Bay region, Silicon Valley, and Sacramento.

The resort is at the site of the historic Kirkwood Inn, built in 1864 as a stop on the Mormon Emigrant Trail over the High Sierra. At a base elevation of 7,800 feet, some 1,600 feet higher than the Lake Tahoe basin, and with a mountain elevation of 9,800 feet, it has one of the region's highest annual snowfalls at an average of 433 inches. The expansiveness of the mountain places Kirkwood among the least crowded mountain resorts in North America at five skiers per acre. Ranked by *Ski* magazine as the number-ten ski resort in the United States, the winter activities have been supplemented by a dedicated program of hiking and mountain biking in the summer, making Kirkwood a successful year-round mountain resort.

LEFT **Single-family homes at Kirkwood; OPPOSITE Skiers at the Mountain Club; horses at the Meadow Trail; summer activities.**

At Cobb's urging, the Telluride Company, where he was a board member, bought into the Kirkwood Mountain Resort in 1994 as part of a plan to establish a portfolio of ski resorts. When Telluride was sold in the late 1990s to a private group, Cobb took his proceeds and bought out the Telluride Company, becoming the major investor through Cobb Partners. He became chairman of the board of Kirkwood Mountain Resort and began a careful upgrade of the resort. He hired Gary Derck from Reno, Nevada, to be CEO of Kirkwood. After Cobb Partners and Gary Engle's company purchased Durango Mountain Ski Resort, Derck became CEO of Durango and Dave Likins became CEO of Kirkwood.

THE MASTER PLAN FOR KIRKWOOD MOUNTAIN RESORT

The original master plan dated to 1972 and had located approximately 1,500 fairly dense mid-rise lodge and condominium units on the resort's main roadway loop. The new owners wanted to change the mix of accommodations to include more townhouses and single-family units and to locate these on the hill to allow ski-in, ski-out access. This new plan traded down the density to get the mix and location the owners believed would produce more sales and revenue and provide a better environment for the community.

Kirkwood has 700 acres of private land, of which 300 acres remain to be developed. The master development plan approved in 2007 set up the village center near the major ski lifts and a lodge in the village

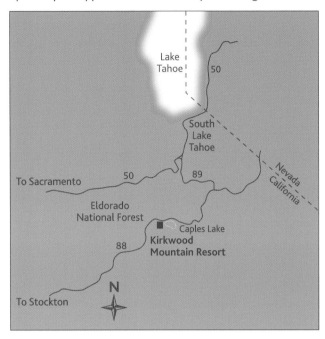

as a central check-in for the entire resort. The resort has a daycare center, a recreation and swim complex, a post office and general store in the Mountain Village, a medical clinic, conference rooms, and 12 diverse lodging properties varying from the restored historic Kirkwood Inn to the Lodge at Kirkwood, condominiums, cabins, and vacation homes. The resort has 474 additional permitted development units for both single-family and mixed-use/multifamily development. The units are spread through four villages, each truly slope side and ski-in, ski-out.

The permits from the U.S. Forest Service run through 2039 for the 2,300 acres operated on Forest Service lands. Extensive environmental and operational policies at Kirkwood ensure the developments harmonize with the natural resources of the Eldorado National Forest and the multiple-use goals of the Forest Service in a sustainable way.

The Kirkwood Community Association provides a wide array of community amenities and year-round activities, property management, and infrastructure maintenance for the resident members of Kirkwood Mountain Resort. The association supports 20 homeowners associations that provide standards for design review of buildings and structures and maintenance of local common amenities. It also provides the community-wide recreation center with pool, spa and fitness facilities, and the Red Cliffs Club, a lounge at the base of the ski lifts.

The Kirkwood Mountain Public Utilities District provides water and sewer, parks, and snow removal for 700 residential customers. The Kirkwood Mountain Resort owns Mountain Utilities, which provides electricity and propane gas for the residents. The resort has entered into an agreement to sell Mountain Utilities to the Kirkwood Mountain Public Utilities District, and the sale is expected to close in 2011. The Kirkwood Volunteer Fire Department provides fire service to the entire resort area.

KIRKWOOD TODAY

Kirkwood attracts 350,000 skiers annually. In the 2009–2010 fiscal year, the resort had record profits buoyed by a strong winter performance along with a noticeable increase in summer revenues. Bucking the trend in U.S. real estate, the resort sold over $30 million of real estate in that year. With prebubble prices of $300,000 for slope-side, ski-in, ski-out single-family lots and fractional ownership of condominiums starting at $20,000, prices at Kirkwood compared favorably to the Tahoe marketplace.

OPPOSITE The historic Kirkwood Inn, now restored; LEFT Summer at Kirkwood; BELOW A new home at Kirkwood.

By virtue of its vast terrain and operational efficiency, Kirkwood has been able to provide value through vacation packages and to take advantage of recent trends that show mountain leisure travelers outspending beach travel by nearly double. Kirkwood has also benefited from trends during the current recession of consumers replacing spending on material objects for spending on experiences such as skiing that create lasting family memories.

These trends apply equally in the summer with respect to the extensive mountain biking and hiking trails served by both lifts and service roads, in easy, more difficult, advanced, and expert categories. Also the regional hiking and backpacking trail systems are well documented from the Kirkwood Meadow to trails overlooking Caples Lake, with connections for the hardy for views to Lake Tahoe and the High Sierras.

Cobb again used an experienced management team to plan, develop, operate, and finance a resort community. With the ability to create high-quality real estate products that meet the family-oriented recreation market and to operate the resort to the satisfaction of both residents and visitors, they use the two revenue streams to maintain a sense of quality and community.

Durango

Mountain Resort

Durango Mountain Resort is located in the beautiful San Juan Mountains of southwest Colorado approximately 25 miles north of the town of Durango. The area was originally called Purgatory by the Spanish in 1776 and then by the silver miners of the 1890s. With a mountain summit of 10,822 feet, a vertical drop of 2,029 feet, and 260 inches of snow annually, the area is considered by serious skiers to be more like heaven than purgatory. Nevertheless, the historic ties to the name were commemorated when the Purgatory ski area was begun by the Duncan family in 1965.

In 2000, Cobb Partners, led by CEO Chuck Cobb, in partnership with Gary Engle, rekindled previous negotiations with the Duncan family to purchase a controlling interest in the 2,500-acre U.S. Forest Service Purgatory ski area and the adjacent 600 acres of private lands. As chairman of Durango Mountain Resort, Cobb brought in Gary Derck as CEO to fulfill his vision of creating a truly unique alpine resort community that offered affordable vacation-home options for southwestern families in a setting that captured the special charm and family friendliness that make Durango and the San Juan Mountains such a popular four-season destination.

Cobb's vision was to first create a unique physical environment that accentuated the spectacular mountain views and felt indigenous with the high-alpine setting, which was created through careful site and architectural design guidelines. Then he and Derck layered a social fabric of inclusive club, community, and resort amenities that accelerated interaction and connection, creating a feeling of "home" for residents. Finally, Cobb created a community finance structure that not only positioned the real estate as a great value, but also kept the ongoing cost of ownership very reasonable.

The community's amenities have been designed to suit the lifestyles of Durango Mountain Resort's residents, with separate villages featuring alpine ski-in, ski-out access, Nordic ski and snowshoe trails, snowmobile garages with direct access to regional snowmobile trails, mountain-bike trails, and lake frontage. The result is one of the most visually stunning and family-friendly mountain resort communities in the West.

LEFT Purgatory Village at the Durango Mountain Resort; **OPPOSITE** Taking a break on the mountain; an all-season resort.

PHOTOGRAPHS OF THIS DEVELOPMENT COURTESY OF DURANGO MOUNTAIN RESORT

131 | COBB'S MASTER-PLANNED COMMUNITIES

THE RESORT ELEMENTS

Durango Mountain Resort has been planned and developed on 600 acres of private land under a 25-year development agreement approved by La Plata and San Juan counties in 2002. The agreement creates the framework for upgraded resort amenities, 1,649 additional residential units, and 410,000 square feet of commercial space with the following key characteristics:

- Clustered village development with six distinct villages on the flatter upland areas, leaving steep slopes, wetlands, and vegetative separations undeveloped between clusters;
- Product diversity with a variety of housing types and prices (from luxury custom homes to fractional slope-side condominiums) and varied commercial, amenity, and support facilities;

LEFT Purgatory Village in the summer; **RIGHT** Homes on the slopes.

- Traffic measures to reduce reliance on automobiles by providing mixed-use commercial areas within walking distance to villages; significant trails for pedestrians, bicycles, and skiers throughout the property; a grade-separated crossing of U.S. Route 550; and regular intra-resort and to/from town shuttle service during peak seasons;
- Customized workforce housing;
- State-of-the-art air quality protection;
- Unique wildlife protection measures with habitat preservation;
- Design and development standards to avoid "skylining" of structures on ridge tops;
- Roads sited to follow natural contours, use building envelopes to precisely locate structures, protect tree cover and minimize visual impact, and promote indigenous and water conserving landscapes; and
- Water conservation built into all domestic and landscape water use standards.

The community features a comprehensive recycling program, a self-improvement and community adventure center (the Durango Mountain Institute), a state-of-the-art telecommunications system, and a year-round medical clinic. The Durango Mountain Master Association (the master homeowners association overseeing 14 individual associations) provides overall governance. Community services and utilities are provided by the Purgatory Metropolitan District and Durango Mountain Utilities.

Cobb and Derck pioneered an upgraded mountain master plan for Purgatory. The ski mountain at Durango Mountain Resort includes numerous environmental mitigation and improvement initiatives to offset any impacts from mountain facilities. These improvements include repairing historical damage from past logging and grazing activities, fencing and revegetation of grazing areas, restoration of stream channels, erosion control, and vegetation management. Biodiesel is used in grooming of the mountain trails and in the resort shuttle fleet. Recycling, green building standards, energy conservation, water conservation, and vehicle mile reduction initiatives are standard operating procedures. The mountain master plan allows the resort to improve lifts, trails, and mountain facilities as the mountain grows to meet the demand from its residents and resort guests. In early 2010, the resort was awarded the National Ski Areas Association Silver Eagle award for excellence in fish and wildlife habitat protection by a ski resort. This is one of the ski industry's highest environmental honors. Durango Mountain Resort was recognized for its comprehensive efforts in planning and implementing the Legends expansion project, which not only increased the resort's total skiable acreage by 10 percent, but also improved forest health and wildlife habitat.

BELOW Changing seasons at Durango Mountain Resort; OPPOSITE Sleigh rides at the village.

PURGATORY VILLAGE AND THE DURANGO MOUNTAIN CLUB

At the heart of Durango Mountain Resort is Purgatory Village, which currently houses 600 condominium units and 60,000 square feet of commercial space with an arrival court, plaza, ski lifts, shopping, and restaurants. It is the central gathering place for the resort and the location of winter and summer concerts, events, and festivals. The village also houses the central check-in for lodging and rental guests. Within the village, the re-

sort offers convenient slope-side accommodations ranging from simple to luxury—and the jewel in the crown is the recently built Purgatory Lodge.

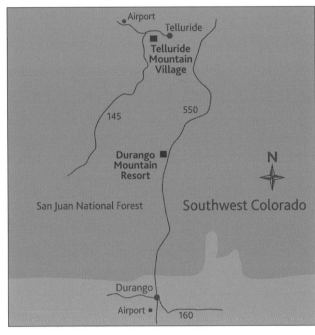

Purgatory Lodge is a combination of fractional-ownership two-, three-, and four-bedroom units as well as a private residence club. Each residence boasts full gourmet kitchens and ski-in, ski-out slope-side access. Owners and guests have access to the Durango Mountain Club—a family-oriented club with social facilities in a private lounge, along with a game room, locker room, fitness center, pool, and spa. Club members include residents of the resort community and local members from nearby Durango.

Durango Mountain Resort operates in all four seasons, but most guests visit during the peak winter and summer seasons. Hiking, mountain biking, and other mountain activities are the main summer attractions. The ski lifts offer scenic rides to the summits. An equestrian center, horseback riding trails, and backpacking open up the mountain terrain. The Alpine Slide and rock climbing are fun ways to experience the San Juan Mountain splendor. Trips to nearby Mesa Verde National Park or a ride on the historic Durango and Silverton Narrow Gauge Railroad round out the activities. The multiple recreation facilities and attractions in nearby Durango are a key reason why 85 percent of visitors return and 90 percent recommend Durango Mountain Resort to their friends.

DURANGO AS A BASE

Durango, Colorado, located 25 miles south of the Durango Mountain Resort on U.S. Route 550, serves as a base for access and services to the resort and offers many additional recreation activities. Frontier, United, and US Airways schedule flights to Durango, and the resort offers shuttle service for its guests to and from town.

The historic Victorian mining town, located on the Animas River, affords access to fly fishing, whitewater rafting, kayaking, and canoeing. The town has winter and summer festivals and multiple golf courses, is the home of Fort Lewis College and state-of-the-art Mercy Regional Medical Center, and has many shops and tourist facilities and more restaurants per capita than San Francisco.

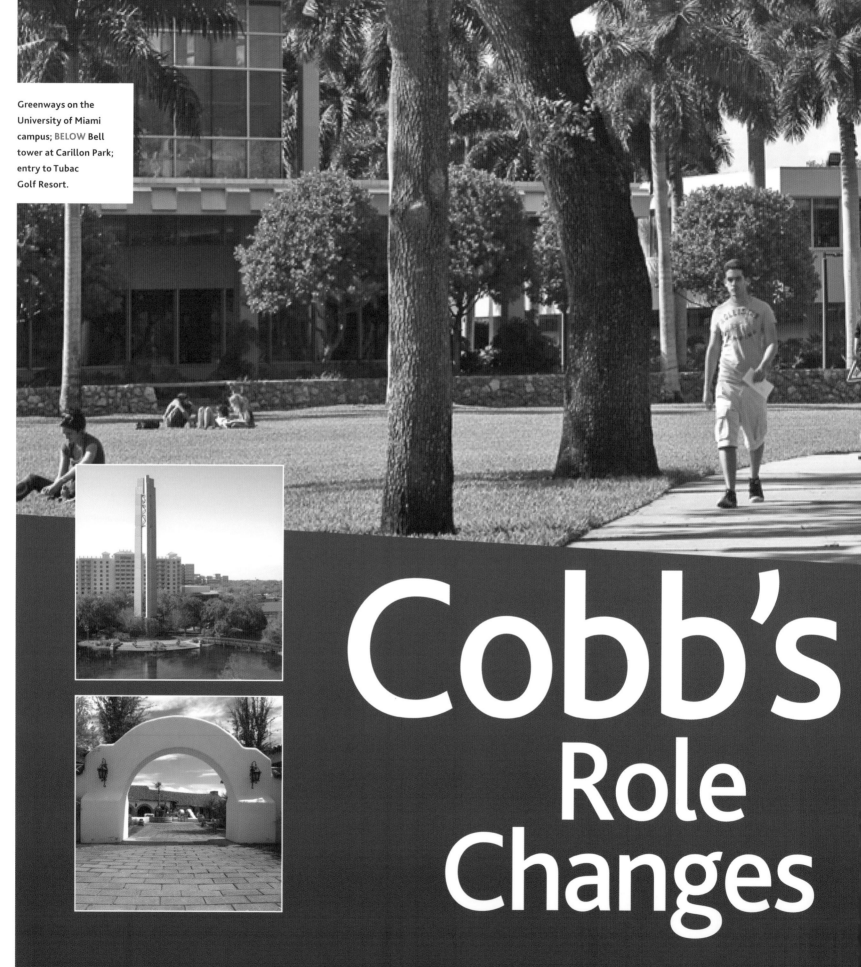

Greenways on the University of Miami campus; BELOW Bell tower at Carillon Park; entry to Tubac Golf Resort.

Cobb's Role Changes

THE MASTER-PLANNED PROJECTS

that follow were developed when Chuck Cobb was not the CEO but a member of the board of the development entity. He makes this careful distinction to give proper credit to those who were more intimately involved with the developments.

Telluride

Ski and Golf Resort

In the mid-1980s, while he was CEO of Arvida Disney, Cobb wanted to buy 50 percent of the Telluride Company to expand the Arvida master-planned communities into destination ski resorts. His reasoning was that government regulations and prohibitive costs would constrain the development of new American ski resorts, which are mostly built on U.S. Forest Service land. More important, Cobb and Arvida Disney had planning, development, and operational skills and experience derived from their many master-planned communities that would directly apply to this kind of resort community. They had the people and organization from Arvida combined with Disney's entertainment capabilities and the development expertise of Ron Allred, the CEO of Telluride.

Cobb thought Telluride was the ideal place to get involved in an existing high-quality ski resort. However, Disney chairman Michael Eisner was concerned that it would be a diversion from the entertainment business, and the deal did not go through.

Cobb left Arvida and Disney in 1987 when he was appointed an assistant secretary and then under secretary of the U.S. Department of Commerce by President Reagan. Later, President George H.W. Bush named him an ambassador for the United States. Before joining the government, Cobb had set up Cobb Partners with some of the key executives who had left Arvida Disney at the same time.

In 1992, after leaving public service and rejoining Cobb Partners, Cobb became an investor and joined the board of directors of Telluride Mountain Resort, determined to bring his experience in master-planned communities to destination mountain resort communities.

LEFT "The G" connecting Telluride Mountain Village to the old town; **OPPOSITE TOP** The historic town of Telluride; in the Mountain Village.

CONNECTING OLD AND NEW AT TELLURIDE

What makes the experience at Telluride unique is its world-class terrain for skiing that catches the spirit of an old-world resort with new-world amenities. The town of Telluride with its historic brick main street and Victorian homes provides the base for festivals and resort services in a spectacular setting against the

COURTESY OF TELLURIDE MOUNTAIN VILLAGE

towering peaks of its box canyon. A significant portion of the town is listed on the National Register of Historic Places.

In 1985, Ron Allred and Jim Wells began building Telluride Mountain Village, a separate incorporated town of 2,500 acres at an elevation of 9,500 feet. Telluride Mountain Village has direct access to a variety of skiing

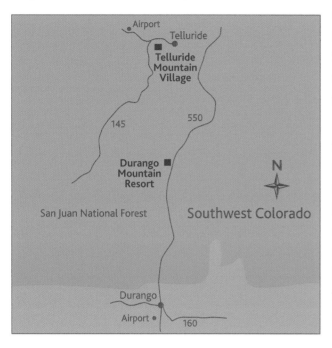

and the ambience of a Swiss alpine village. In addition, it is a compact, walkable destination with luxury hotels, a conference center, and year-round activities such as golf, mountain biking, and hiking.

A comprehensive, free transportation system enables residents and visitors to get around without clogging the villages with cars. The two resort villages are connected by a gondola, called "the G," which has four stops serving the towns and recreational facilities. Thus the major transportation mode between the two resort bases offers a spectacular experience in itself. The two villages are also connected by road transportation.

The gondola stops at an interceptor parking deck at Telluride Mountain Village. A shuttle serves the gondola and loops around the town and has dial-a-ride within the village areas.

MOVING ON TO MULTIPLE SKI RESORTS

In 1994, the Telluride Company began looking into acquiring other destination ski resorts in line with Cobb's view of the future difficulties of building new resorts. The company bought an interest in Kirkwood Mountain Resort in California and began negotiating with the Durango Mountain Resort south of Telluride. In the late 1990s, Telluride was sold out to a private group. Cobb took his proceeds from this sale and bought out Telluride's interest in Kirkwood and purchased an interest in Durango, which enabled him to realize his vision of being more directly involved with multiple destination resorts.

Telluride was the launching pad for Cobb's role as an investor and board member who was intimately involved in the community development process in mountain resorts. Although the new role was different, the process and the technology were similar. He applied the same smart growth development principles to these mountain communities that he had used so successfully in his other developments.

OPPOSITE, TOP The Telluride Mountain Village Center; OPPOSITE, BOTTOM The Westermere at the Mountain Village.

Tubac

Golf Resort and Spa

LEFT The resort core; OPPOSITE, TOP Entry to the Tubac Resort; the historic Otero House, restored as a conference center; RIGHT Golfing at Tubac.

PHOTOGRAPHS OF THIS DEVELOPMENT COURTESY OF TUBAC GOLF RESORT AND SPA

Established in 1752 as a Spanish Presidio, Tubac was the first European settlement in Arizona. Don Toribio de Otero received from the king of Spain the first land grant in what is now the southwestern United States for his 500-acre ranch just north of the village of Tubac. The master-planned community, Tubac Golf Resort and Spa, is located on this historic ranch.

Located in Santa Cruz County, Arizona, 40 miles south of Tucson and 20 miles north of the Mexican border on I-19, Tubac's elevation of 3,500 feet provides a more temperate climate than Tucson. With its rich history and art scene, the town is home to some 1,000 permanent residents. It is the starting point of Juan Bautista de Anza National Historic Trail to California and the site of Tubac Presidio State Historic Park, Tubac Center of the Arts, and Tubac Festival of the Arts.

The town has more than 90 shops and galleries in a relaxed, authentic old-town Arizona atmosphere. It includes 13 restaurants, a market, a community center, and medical facilities and has no traffic lights. The many annual festivals, the mountain climate, and the shopping attract visitors from across the southwest.

Originally established in 1959 as an 18-hole golf course with homesites, Tubac was purchased in 2000 by Ron Allred, Jim Wells, and some of their partners at Telluride Ski and Golf Resort, including Chuck Cobb. They set the policies and made the necessary investments to transform the property into the Tubac Golf Resort and Spa community. Today it features a 27-hole championship golf course with practice facilities, a clubhouse and pro shop, and a 4,000-square-foot spa and fitness center with a tennis court and heated swimming pool. Other facilities include three full-service restaurants, a 7,000-square-foot conference center, and 98 guest accommodations in casitas, suites, and hotel rooms. Otero House, the historic former home of the Otero family, has been restored and made into executive quarters and small meeting rooms.

Fronting the golf course and adjacent to the lush, vegetated courses of the Santa Cruz River are a custom-homebuilder development and individual sites for custom homes ranging in size from one-quarter to one-half acre. The golf course extends south to the edge of Tubac Village, and the hotel is three-quarters of a mile to the village on Burruel Street. The Juan Bautista de Anza National Historic Trail begins in the village; it is approximately one mile on the trail from the Presidio State Historic Park to the Tubac resort.

Cobb's long experience planning and developing master-planned communities as a CEO enabled him in the fiduciary role as an owner and board member to work with his partners and Tubac's CEO to take the project from a simple golf subdivision to a master-planned resort community. The team used its combination of re-sort operations and real estate development skills to make this resort a success.

OPPOSITE **The 18th hole of the Tubac Golf Course; BELOW Dining at the resort.**

In doing so, the Tubac resort community also became a model of smarter, more sustainable development. The original subdivision was enhanced with a hotel with full resort facilities and conference capabilities that blended well with the many events and high visitation in the adjacent village. Strong pedestrian connections were created between the village and the resort. Housing choices were increased by adding builder housing and haciendas or villas to the lot sales programs. The resort core with shops, restaurants, and a chapel formed a compact center, easily walkable from the hotel villas. Large conservation areas were extended along the Santa Cruz River, providing natural recreational areas and scenic surroundings for residents and visitors.

Carillon Park

Carillon Park is a 432-acre mixed-use development in the Gateway business district of the Tampa Bay metropolitan area. The development is equidistant from the central business districts of Tampa, St. Petersburg, and Clearwater and close to the St. Petersburg and Tampa International airports. The property was purchased in the late 1980s by Echelon Real Estate Company, a public company listed on the New York Stock Exchange.

Echelon provided a high-quality infrastructure for Carillon with a roadway network connecting to major arterials and I-275, complete underground utilities, street lighting, and signage throughout. A significant feature is the 100-acre wetland conservation area with boardwalks, a jogging trail, and several large lakes. A signature carillon bell tower is featured on the central lake, and all roads and common areas are landscaped at the highest standards.

The strategic location and high development standards of Carillon attracted major office facilities of Raymond James Financial, Allstate, Franklin Templeton Funds, and Aegon-Western Reserve Life. Carillon Park

COURTESY OF CARILLON PARK

COURTESY OF CARILLON PARK

LEFT Bell tower and hotel at the central pond; OPPOSITE Aerial view of Carillon looking toward Tampa Bay.

includes 3.2 million square feet of office development, a 227-room Hilton Hotel (located on the bell tower pond), and the 145,000-square-foot St. Anthony's Carillon Wellness Center with medical offices, trauma center, and outpatient surgery center.

Cobb became a shareholder in Echelon when a group of other shareholders and fellow board members, including his previous partners Gary Engle and Jim Coyne, took over the public company in the early 2000s.

As a member of the board he worked with CEO Darryl LeClair to reestablish Carillon by converting Echelon into a smaller private company, by selling off assets other than Carillon, and by using the proceeds to reduce debt and to focus on realizing the mixed-use potential of this well-located property, thereby transforming it into a vital master-planned community.

Carillon is now planned to include a mix of employment and housing in an environment suitable for both. Carillon received two Development of Regional Impact (DRI) approvals, as required under Florida statutes. One covered the western, primarily office portion of the community, and the other covered primarily the eastern town center and residential portion. The two DRIs allow a total of 6 million square feet of office space and 1,500 multifamily rental or ownership residential units.

Currently, in addition to the office development, the eastern portion of Carillon has 930 units of rental apartments and for-sale villas. The residences are surrounded by lakes and conservation areas and served by a state-of-the-art fitness center and a convenience retail center anchored by a Publix supermarket.

Under development is a pedestrian-friendly town center with a mix of uses that include retail, entertainment, office, residential, hotel, and structured parking. The buildings will cluster along a main street, and the town center will become the downtown for the entire Carillon community. These new elements will make Carillon a fully integrated master-planned community where people can live, work, and play.

In addition to making the property more economically viable, the transformation brought Carillon more in line with smart growth principles. It fully implemented the mix of land uses to include jobs and housing; extended pedestrian systems connecting the different uses and preserves; continued a strong identity with creative landscapes, a series of ponds, preserved wetlands, and environmental areas; created a new compact, walkable town center; and took advantage of the excellent transportation systems in the Gateway region of the Tampa Bay metropolitan area.

Carillon's transformation received critical guidance from Cobb and his partners, who brought years of experience in planning and developing master-planned communities to this strategic property. They began by changing Echelon, making reinvestment possible and refocusing on the full potential of Carillon as a complete master-planned community.

Office building with pond in foreground.

WCI Master-Planned

Based in Bonita Springs, Florida, WCI is a homebuilder known for its more than 50 amenity-rich master-planned communities serving primary, retirement, and second-home buyers. The communities have a lifestyle orientation with golf, tennis, walking trails, and spas and have won many awards. The residential units range in price from the low $100,000s to more than $3 million (2010 dollars).

In 2005, Al Hoffman, the founder and CEO of WCI, asked Chuck Cobb to join the board of WCI and to eventually become the chairman until Hoffman returned from being U.S. Ambassador to Portugal. Cobb was elected vice chairman, but before he could be elevated to chairman, Carl Icahn bought 30 percent of WCI stock and in a legal settlement became chairman with Cobb remaining on the board for several years and then resigning. WCI was then reorganized in bankruptcy court. Even with its financial difficulties, WCI managed to build more than 50 significant master-planned communities. Three examples described here are typical of the projects developed by WCI.

TIBURON

Tiburon is a resort community that effectively blends a luxury resort hotel with a lifestyle community. The Ritz-Carlton Golf Resort at Naples, Florida, shares recreational amenities with the residents of Tiburon. They include two Greg Norman golf courses and a 27,000-square-foot golf club, tennis courts, fitness and spa facilities, beach transport, and club member concierge services. Residential products include a range of golf course–frontage homes, estate homesites, and condominiums. Several hundred acres of conservation areas in Tiburon provide a green environment for the resort and community.

Tiburon is three and a half miles from the Gulf Coast beaches and six and a half miles from Naples and Naples Municipal Airport. It has convenient access to I-75 and the Southwest Florida International Airport and Fort Myers to the north.

RIGHT **Architectural details at the Tiburon Club; OPPOSITE, TOP TO BOTTOM Homes on the Colony Golf Course; condominiums on the golf course and lakes at Old Palm; Tiburon Golf Club, fitness, and health club.**

Communities

BONITA SPRINGS, FLORIDA

A developer and builder of master-planned communities

OLD PALM GOLF CLUB

Old Palm Golf Club is a private golf club in the heart of Palm Beach Gardens, north of Palm Beach and West Palm Beach, in southeastern Florida. It consists of 651 acres, 125 existing luxury residences, sites for 145 additional homes, a Raymond Floyd golf course featuring a 33-acre practice and training facility, and a 43,000-square-foot clubhouse. Located on PGA Boulevard, Old Palm Golf Club is only a few miles from the PGA (Professional Golf Association) National Headquarters.

The homes in Old Palm feature architecture based on the legendary style of Addison Mizner, architect and developer of Palm Beach and Boca Raton. Homes, golf villas, and custom homesites line the golf course. Lots vary in size from one-quarter to one acre. Waterways and oak and pine hammock preserves add interest and environmental values to the golf course and community. Raymond Floyd believes Old Palm is one of the best golf courses he has designed.

THE COLONY GOLF AND BAY CLUB

The Colony, in Bonita Springs, Florida, is an approximately 1,000-acre community fully entitled for 1,600 units around a championship Jerry Pate–designed golf course and 28,000-square-foot country club. The Bay Club overlooks Estero Bay, and major areas are devoted to shoreline preserves and wetlands. The community is approximately 50 percent built out.

Residences include several types of high-rise, mid-rise, and low-rise condominiums, golf-frontage houses, and golf villas. There is a Hyatt Regency Resort and Spa, a community spa and fitness center, and the Pelican Landing Tennis Center. The community has rights to Beach Park, fronting on the Gulf of Mexico, and shuttle service to the beach.

FINANCING MASTER-PLANNED COMMUNITIES

Master-planned communities need to be financed for the long run to weather the long periods necessary to build real community with the attendant risks of up and down markets. Developers typically face seven- to 25-year buildout periods for these communities. The extraordinary heights of the real estate market in 2005 seemed to render that maxim not applicable. WCI management proposed and then exchanged high-interest unsecured debt for low-interest debt with strict bank covenants. These covenants could not be met in 2007, and WCI's board concluded that bankruptcy was the best course of action. Even though the banks now have a high percentage of ownership in these communities, they have maintained their desirability, and as WCI has come out of bankruptcy, it has returned to the business of developing master-planned communities.

OPPOSITE **The golf studio at Old Palm Golf Course;** LEFT **Houses on the Old Palm Golf Course;** BELOW **Condominiums at the Colony Tennis Center.**

The lesson is that well-planned community development involves very long time frames and therefore depends on financial structures that allow debt to be serviced in bad times as well as good. In this case, Cobb, as a member of the board, was not successful in getting WCI to follow this long-standing principle of master-planned community development.

University

# of Miami Campus

In 1975, following his long-term interest in education, Cobb became a trustee of the University of Miami. He has served on the board for more than 30 years as a member, as chairman, on the executive committee, and as head of several other committees. In his capacities as the chairman of the master planning and construction committee during the 1980s and 1990s, he was able to apply his experience in creating master-planned communities to this academic community. In the early 1980s, a new university president, Edward T. Foote II, was selected by Cobb and other search committee members partially for the strategic planning orientation he shared with Cobb. Foote had the will and desire to finally bring the physical as well as the academic environment of the Coral Gables campus up to its potential and to truly reflect the university's impressive growth and excellence. President Foote recognized the potential jewel he had in this great new university, set in the exotic subtropics and in a region fast becoming the center of inter-American learning and culture.

LEFT The library grove of royal palms; OPPOSITE, TOP Students on the greenways; the academic core.

The University of Miami was founded in 1925 in Coral Gables, "the City Beautiful," with a donation of 160 acres by George Merrick, the city's visionary developer. Merrick's goal, cited in his original master plan, was "to establish Coral Gables as the educational center of the South and the natural meeting place of the culture of North America, Central America, and South America." After a long and rocky road from 1926 when the first students arrived, more than 50 years were needed to fulfill that vision. Today, with 15,000 students, the university has become the largest private educational institution in the southeastern United States. It includes schools of law, medicine, engineering, education, architecture, music, nursing, marine science, business, and arts and sciences.

MASTER-PLANNING AN ACADEMIC COMMUNITY

In the early 1980s, the Coral Gables main campus of 250 acres showed the results of discontinuous, then rapid growth. It lacked overall identity, cohesiveness, and quality, except in a few special areas. The campus had a good basic structure. It was bounded on all sides by public roads with access to mostly peripheral parking areas, an academic core, supporting special uses, student residential areas, athletic fields, and a student center on the seven-acre Lake Osceola. Most parts of the campus were within a ten-minute walk of one another.

Early campus plans determined no vehicles or parking lots would be in the core, so it could be a pedestrian precinct. This plan was most notoriously violated by a faculty parking area in the center of the academic core between the main library, administration building, and classroom buildings.

Another problem was that entry to the core for visitors was from the south at Stanford Drive near Dixie Highway, which did not provide a direct and easily understood access to the administration building, academic core, or library. Moreover, very little other than Lake Osceola and the student center gave the campus any common areas of distinction or connection to its climate or its distinctive setting in the sylvan neighborhoods of Coral Gables.

President Foote had a vision of "a campus in a tropical garden." This vision became the primary goal of the first element of a new university plan, a *Landscape and Urban Design Plan* prepared by the SWA Group and Walter Taft Bradshaw, published and quickly implemented by the Cobb-led master-planning committee. The first phase, in 1983, was to build the infrastructure so that the new president's vision could begin to take shape. New academic buildings and campus facilities quickly followed.

The first phase of construction transformed Memorial Drive from a small road that provided access from the northwest peripheral roadway into a memorable major entry statement to befit its role as a major access to the academic core, library, and administration building. The entry with its coral rock walls, lush, tropical plantings, stone pavements, and special lighting fixtures was easily located by visitors. Cobb had used these types of features in all his planned communities to create places of distinction and beauty.

The faculty parking lot was removed from its site on the central green, and the area was transformed into a continuous open space that connected the university arboretum on the north edge of the academic core to the student center and Lake Osceola on the south. Memorial Drive was shortened and now terminates on a multifunctional plaza that serves as a turnaround for the university shuttle buses. In the center of the plaza is a large fountain framed by a grove of royal palms that provides shade for seating and pedestrian areas. The royal palm is a signature tree for the University of Miami because it cannot flourish anywhere in the mainland

LEFT The main campus of the University of Miami in Coral Gables; RIGHT The University Fountain in the Royal Palm Court.

United States outside of south Florida, and its majestic form and height make it an appropriate image for the subtropical educational institution.

Very quickly, the royal palms and fountain in the center of the expanded academic core became the symbol of the University of Miami on television and in print. To replace the faculty parking lot, underused peripheral parking lots were improved with heavy shade-tree plantings. They were connected to the core campus with wide walkways that branched out from the plaza. These walkways were also lined with rows of royal palms. Even though faculty members were told before the summer break of the plan to relocate the parking, they revolted about having to walk this small additional distance, which in turn led to the planners' removal from the next phases of campus redevelopment.

In later phases, a broad palm-lined walkway with outdoor cafés was extended to connect the library to the student center. Cobb donated a 40-foot-high fountain to be installed in Lake Osceola to provide a focal point for the south campus and to help transport oxygen to the deep lake waters. The "campus in a tropical garden" had taken a permanent hold.

THE UNIVERSITY OF TOMORROW

With more than 15,000 students from around the world, the University of Miami has been ranked among the top tier of national universities by *U.S. News and World Report*. It has five campuses with celebrated theater and music programs, museums, and intercollegiate athletics. Chuck Cobb sponsored the Cobb Stadium for Soccer, Track and Field at the Coral Gables campus to commemorate his record-breaking high hurdles career when at Stanford University and in the U.S. Navy. He also spearheaded the development of a 32-acre residential community with 30 houses for faculty at the Smathers Four Fillies Farm several miles south of the campus. This development won the 2009 Woolbright Dream Green Reality Award, given by the Urban Land Institute's Southeast Florida/Caribbean District Council for sustainable development practices.

OPPOSITE View of the southern edge of the campus with Metrorail and Dixie Highway connecting to the city of Miami in the distance; **LEFT** Connecting the student center to the library.

Cobb saw the potential redevelopment opportunities in a 60-acre area on the south side of the campus where a series of 1950s-era residence halls had become physically and functionally obsolete. Once again, his experience in master-planned community development aided greatly in setting flexible but realistic guidelines for this new part of the campus. The plan was to keep the academic core at the north end of the campus as compact as possible, so this area would be redeveloped mostly with residential and university support facilities. More public-oriented uses would be located toward the southern edge facing the Miami Metrorail station and Dixie Highway. Cobb and the SWA design team saw the site offering the university a 21st-century opportunity to create a transit-oriented development on the campus that would serve all of metropolitan Dade County.

The first redevelopment project was the Bank United Convocation Center, a much-needed facility for functions and athletic events. The site's convenient access made it a good location for this facility, because it would hold events open to the public. A parking and shuttle-bus garage followed on the southwest periphery near the Convocation Center and close to the Metrorail station, offering easy train, bus, and parking connections. The land directly across from the Metrorail station was recently designated for a major health care facility for residents of South Miami and the Coral Gables area. The facility is sponsored by the University Medical School, which is located off campus, at Jackson Memorial Hospital near downtown Miami. Because the Metrorail station at the Coral Gables campus connects directly to a station at Jackson Memorial, this new health care facility will allow quick transit connections between the two for doctors and medical students, and it will open easy access for the entire Metrorail system.

Cobb's strategic planning skills were put to good use at the university. In his role as a board member, he provided analysis of the best land uses, focused on infrastructure and transportation, ensured architectural and landscape controls, and helped develop a good master plan for the campus. In 2001, President Foote was replaced by a new president, Donna Shalala. Policies implemented by Shalala and her staff furthered Cobb's smart growth goals: increased transit use and transportation choice, easy pedestrian access to the compact academic core and supporting facilities, a protected open space and greenway system throughout the campus, a mix of university and public-serving uses, and a distinctive sense of place.

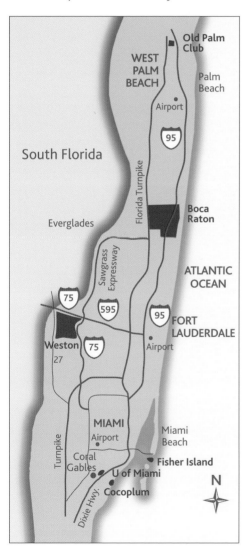

RIGHT Estates and open-space preserves at Rancho California; BELOW Tournament Players Club at Sawgrass; landscaped road-ways in Boca Raton.

Lessons Learned

Cobb's Master-Planned Communities and Smart Growth

THE COMMUNITIES EXAMINED

in this book are evaluated in terms of two key factors.
First, did they create economically and environmentally sound communities and a desirable quality of life
in an overall sense? The short answer, apparent even
from a cursory review of the accompanying texts and
photographs, is a resounding yes. All these pioneering master-planned communities—some begun more
than 45 years ago—are today vital, economically and

environmentally successful, and sought-after places to live, work, and enjoy life. Whereas traditional suburban sprawl becomes worn looking and outdated in only a few decades, the Cobb communities have remained attractive and desirable over the years, and they readily attract homebuyers and commercial investors who maintain and make continued upgrades to the properties. Thus, these communities offer proven lessons on what works for large-scale development over the long term that is helpful in planning for smart growth today. In Cobb's words, "We set the mark for nearby parks, schools, jobs, shops, and strong community identity—it used to be the exception but it soon became what was necessary, and everyone was imitating Arvida communities—the philosophy of the consumer changed."

The second criterion is whether Cobb's communities pioneered smart growth. This answer, likewise, is yes—but with some qualifications. In the accompanying table on pages 164–167, three communities that were planned and begun in the 1960s through 1980s are examined in terms of how they exemplify the Smart Growth Network's ten Smart Growth Principles adopted in 1996.

Of particular note, these three Cobb communities achieved nearly all of the smart growth principles, showing the community value and financial practicality of such actions. These master-planned communities mixed a variety of property types (including ample workplaces), used cluster development, created neighborhoods and villages with a range of housing types, provided cost-effective infrastructure and services for residents and businesses, and created a strong and market-proven sense of place. Protected open space and environmentally critical areas were set aside as part of—or in most cases—adjacent to these communities. Finally, local governments were involved as major stakeholders in the planning, approvals, and development decision process.

The shortcomings of these communities in meeting the smart growth principles are apparent in two categories. The first is the limited range of transportation choices, particularly the lack of mass transit, and the lower density and coarser mix of land uses, which, of course, hindered the feasibility of transit and walkability. The second is the uneven availability of affordable housing and in some cases the complete lack of such housing in communities that were targeted to the upper third of the housing market. These shortcomings are further addressed in this chapter.

OPPOSITE **The Arvida Park of Commerce and the Broken Sound Country Club community are linked by the two Broken Sound golf courses; RIGHT Weston was developed as a new town with a town center, landscaped roads and waterways, employment areas, and a variety of residential villages.**

At the time Cobb developed these communities, these particular shortcomings were difficult, if not impossible, for any developer to overcome. Massive federal and state expenditures funded the roadways and other infrastructure for an automobile-dominant transportation system. Local transit was scarce or nonexistent, and some communities feared that higher density would attract the "wrong kind of people." Local governments discouraged and often excluded multifamily development that could have increased density, thus reducing car dependency and establishing one foundation for eventual transit.

Neither federal housing nor home-lending policies strongly targeted housing affordability, and nearly all developers focused on the ownership of increasingly large single-family homes and low-density development whether in a master-planned community or not. Zoning in most jurisdictions restricted the close mixing of uses. In particular, lending institutions would not finance mixed-use buildings or a fine grain of different uses within a neighborhood, even if the jurisdiction permitted such development. Even insurance companies were hurdles to such development practices.

Because of significant changes in local policies and some dramatic shifts in housing markets in the early years of the 21st century, the three communities in the table—Rancho California, Boca Raton, and Weston—are now able to implement new development strategies as they complete their buildout and redevelop underused sites. These strategies include new codes to encourage higher-density, finer-grain mixed-use districts, planning and financing for transit infrastructure, and "complete street" designs to tame automobile traffic and improve walkability and biking. The local jurisdictions for these communities are using inclusive zoning, mandated jobs/housing balance, and new ways to improve housing affordability.

No developer or local community, however, can fully realize all the smart growth principles without changes in the nation's energy and development policies that are more supportive of greener, lower-carbon initiatives; less automobile-centric transportation funding; and real estate lending policies that support greater density, diversity, and more mixed-use projects. Without these significant national, state, and regional as well as lending policy changes, the new local policies will still not allow either existing or newer master-planned communities to fully achieve the smart growth principles. These communities still will not reduce automobile dependency

Three Master-Planned Communities That Exemplify Ten Smart Growth Principles

Rancho California, Temecula and Riverside County (1964)

Weston, Broward County, Florida (1974)

1. MIX OF LAND USES

- City of Temecula with full urban services; complete mix of residential, commercial, industrial, public, and institutional land uses

- Jobs/housing balance: Population 110,000/Jobs 35,000

- Large productive vineyard, citrus and avocado orchards; open-space preserves

- Incorporated in 1996 as the city of Weston with a full mix of land uses, services, and facilities

- Jobs/housing balance: Population 65,000/Jobs 25,000–30,000

- Large wetland and Everglades conservation areas; Cleveland Clinic of Florida

2. COMPACT BUILDING DESIGN

- 90 percent of population occupies 20 percent of land

- Overall Temecula at 6.2 persons per acre compares favorably to new urbanist communities such as Stapleton/Denver at 6.1–7.7 persons per acre

- 23,500 dwelling units: 78 percent single family, 22 percent multifamily

- Population density: 5.75 persons per acre

3. RANGE OF HOUSING OPPORTUNITIES

- 34 percent townhouses and multifamily

- Overall housing mix: ten- to 40-acre estates, one to four units per acre single family, six to ten units per acre small lot or townhouses, 20 units per acre multifamily buildings

- Timeshares, apartments, townhouses, single-family houses, and luxury estates

- Use of different builders for blocks of land to ensure diverse housing design and types

- Rated one of the best affordable suburbs in the United States by *Business Week* in 2006

4. WALKABLE NEIGHBORHOODS

- Series of villages with landscaped sidewalks and paths connecting to schools, parks, and neighborhood commercial

- Newer villages (Harveston) with narrower streets, fine-grained land use, and pedestrian systems that connect to nearby jobs and commercial uses

- Series of villages with sidewalks and shade trees on all streets to enhance walking to six neighborhood elementary schools

- Weston Town Center has mixed uses and narrow, pedestrian-friendly streets

Arvida at Boca Raton, Boca Raton and Palm Beach County, Florida (1972)

- Town center complex, large business park, and expanded Boca Raton Hotel as three core subareas of current city plan to promote mixed use

- Jobs/housing imbalance: Population: 90,000/Jobs: 90,000

- Labor force of only 40,000 compensated for somewhat by large areas of county residential development

- Overall density of 4.3 persons per acre increased to 5.6 persons per acre with the annexation of the denser Arvida Villages

- Residential village design used cluster development; office and business developments clustered into campuses to facilitate connectivity

- Housing densities from one to 3.5 units/acre for single family to five to 9.5 units/acre for townhouses, villas, and low rise, to 20 units/acre for high rise

- Established local qualified builders contracted to meet varied housing needs, and in-house builder for market not served by local builders

- City's low density mandate makes housing costs considerably higher in Boca Raton than Palm Beach County as a whole

- Series of villages with sidewalks, shade trees, and trails connecting to schools, parks, and local commercial facilities

- City is expanding systems with higher service standards and a mixed-use district to facilitate transit, bicycling, and walking as viable options

or serve all markets and demographics or be as green as they could be or offer a mix that includes smaller, more affordable housing.

With the completed communities featured in this book, Chuck Cobb and his teams have proven that the use of smart growth principles can be profitable and thereby provide additional impetus for the growing acceptance of these environmentally supportive and community-enhancing standards. These pioneering communities set the stage for smart growth a generation before the term was invented. Both their successes and shortcomings can provide lessons for any developer or community wanting to plan or carry out more sustainable projects. The successes provide practical and time-proven best practices, while the shortcomings offer useful information on some of the challenges that exist even today in fully meeting these principles.

STRATEGIC PUBLIC AND PRIVATE PLANNING

Neither the public nor the private sector acts alone in creating communities. Cobb's master-planned communities—like most real estate development—are private ventures. Smart growth principles were established by a network of government agencies and nonprofits (including the Urban Land Institute) to provide a framework for better development practices. The master-planned communities of the 1960s and 1970s preceded the smart growth principles by three decades but depend on the collaborative and effective public/private planning process those principles prescribe.

Cobb participated in this public/private synergy in the 1960s when the city of Scottsdale, Arizona, used the process originated at McCormick Ranch as a blueprint to guide its substantial growth for the next

BELOW Storm washes at the McCormick Ranch were planned to also be pedestrian ways.

Rancho California	Weston

5. DISTINCTIVE, ATTRACTIVE COMMUNITIES WITH A STRONG SENSE OF PLACE

Rancho California	Weston
■ All streets, roads, and civic uses have strong landscape elements and streetscape	■ Sixty miles of visually distinctive greenways, and extensive, visually distinctive landscaping
■ Natural elements (mountains, drainage ways, and other physical features) are reinforced in the community design	■ Weston Town Center provides a focus for the community with an exciting sense of place
■ Design controls used throughout for fences, entries, graphics, and all residential, commercial, and industrial uses	■ Design guidelines used in the development of all residential and commercial buildings

6. PRESERVED OPEN SPACE, FARMLAND, NATURAL BEAUTY, AND CRITICAL ENVIRONMENTAL AREAS

Rancho California	Weston
■ 8,200-acre Santa Rosa Plateau Environmental Preserve	■ 320 acres of city parkland and 102-acre regional park with an ancient burial mound
■ 8,850-acre Vail Lake Open Space and Recreation Preserve	■ 1,800 acres in waterways, lakes, and riparian vegetation
■ 7,500-acre Citrus, Vineyard Protection Policy Area	■ 2,000 acres of wetland preservation permanently set aside
■ 3,000-acre Equestrian Policy Area to protect equestrian facilities and estates	■ 4,000 acres designated agricultural, most as wetlands or components of the Comprehensive Everglades Restoration Plan
■ 80 percent of Rancho California area in large-lot estates, agriculture, and open space	

7. DEVELOPMENT ENCOURAGED NEAR EXISTING COMMUNITIES

Rancho California	Weston
■ Temecula Old Town included in and preserved as Historic Temecula District with new civic center attracting appropriate mixed-use development	■ Entire 10,000-acre Weston master-planned community incorporated as the new city of Weston

8. VARIETY OF TRANSPORTATION CHOICES

Rancho California	Weston
■ At the time of the plan, I-15 opened and transportation within the community and to the Los Angeles metropolitan area was primarily by automobile; very little transit service or other choices existed	■ Developed to take advantage of three just-completed region-serving freeways bordering site; access was and still is overwhelmingly by automobile
■ The 21st century has introduced choice beyond a few bus routes, including trolley service to key city areas, and the Temecula/Murrieta joint transit center under development adjacent to a proposed California high-speed-rail station	■ No nearby rail corridors; only one bus route through the city; long-range transit plans very limited and focus on I-75 as a future high-capacity transit corridor
	■ 46 miles of bicycle trails

9. DEVELOPMENT DECISIONS PREDICTABLE, FAIR, AND COST-EFFECTIVE

Rancho California	Weston
■ Rancho California Master Plan cited as the basis for the current city and county land use plans, which enjoy wide public support	■ Planning occurred over five years and involved a Development of Regional Impact study
■ Rancho California Water District is today an efficient public utility serving the entire area	■ Indian Trace Community Development District formed to provide advantageous financing of infrastructure for the community
■ Community associations created by Rancho California continue with wide support to control and maintain large county areas of the plan	■ Still the lowest combined property tax rate in Broward County

10. STAKEHOLDER PARTICIPATION IN DEVELOPMENT DECISIONS

Rancho California	Weston
■ Although not many people lived in the area during its early planning and development phase, strong citizen support exists for the basic elements of the Rancho California Planned Community	■ When the Indian Trace Community Development District that was established by Arvida held an election for incorporation into the new city of Weston, the vote was 90 percent in favor
	■ When Bonaventure, the smaller adjacent community, voted to join Weston, the vote was 2 to 1 in favor

Arvida at Boca Raton

- Landscaped three miles of the state road connecting I-95 to the Florida Turnpike

- All residential and commercial villages have a signature graphic identity system with landscaped walls, berms, entries, graphics, parks, streets, and water management lakes to create attractive settings

- Design controls cover village layout, architecture, and landscape review

- From 30 to 50 percent of the Villages land area is greenways, parks, lakes, golf courses, and environmental preserves

- The city has 1,265 acres of developed parkland and 410 acres of conservation areas, including several miles of beach frontage

- 3,575 acres of the Villages of Arvida developed within the city of Boca Raton or in the county adjacent to the city and later annexed

- 1,425 acres remaining in Palm Beach County directly abut city limits

- Developed to take advantage of newly built I-95 and the extension of the Florida Turnpike; access within the community and to the Florida Gold Coast primarily by automobile with very little transit service

- The 21st century has seen better bus service and establishment of the Tri-Rail station at the Park of Commerce; multiple shuttles, proposed new passenger-rail service on Florida East Coast Rail corridor, bus rapid transit, and local shuttle routes

- Community associations continue to serve their local resident and business communities efficiently and effectively to maintain and control landscape, graphics, recreational amenities, and new construction and renovation

- City of Boca Raton has a complete and transparent development and design control system within its jurisdiction and has annexed most of the Villages of Arvida

- Arvida's planning process involved the elaborate use of illustrative plans, photographs, and charts to communicate the plan concepts to the city and county in many public meetings with the jurisdictions involved

- The government and citizens of Boca Raton and southeastern Palm Beach County were heavily involved in the planning and implementation of the Villages of Arvida

decades. By insisting that future development follow this process, the city ensured that growth occurred primarily through a series of master-planned communities.

Cobb recognized the need for collaborative public/private planning in Florida, where he first worked in 1972. At the time, he was the only major real estate developer to support Governor Reubin Askew's Development of Regional Impact legislation. He did so even though it would require his as well as all future large projects to undergo a long and costly environmental, planning, and infrastructure review and approvals process. The creation of the town of Weston in the 1970s using the Development of Regional Impact process as a public/private planning effort led to a better outcome for both Broward County and Cobb's Arvida Corporation: a well-planned, high-quality, and efficiently publicly financed and managed new city (see Weston case study).

ABOVE Weston was planned as a new town under a Florida Development of Regional Impact procedure.

Cobb's early embrace of this kind of public/private planning came from his interest in strategic planning as a way to get complex things done successfully. It was a way to identify objectives, measure assets and liabilities, and create organizations and methods to achieve the desired results.

Cobb used strategic planning to create the organizations for multiple, large-scale real estate developments. His organizations hired the best people, giving them autonomy and flexibility under the corporate umbrella of the "Cobb Web" (see feature box on page 5). Such planning enabled him to

operate successfully in many locations, over many decades, while facing continuous change in markets, government policies, lending policies, and his various companies' objectives.

Cobb and his team members used strategic planning in the pursuit of a market-driven planning and development process that would meet his business and financial objectives for each master-planned community, while still supporting the longer-term goals stated in the local jurisdiction's comprehensive plans. By creating a corporate organization with a complete set of community-building skills, Cobb rejected advice when he became CEO of Arvida in 1972 to follow then-customary Florida development trends for rapid-profit land sales and short horizons. The communities that he developed in Florida and elsewhere had an average 15-year buildout horizon that served as a middle range between simple subdivisions of land and the 20- to 25-year time span of most public comprehensive plans.

Working with local governments, his team strategically master planned all future development, community facilities and amenities, infrastructure, and recreational clubs to fit into the public planning process. The Cobb teams backed up this longer-term perspective with homeowners and community associations, utility and service districts, and clubs that had both the financial and organizational capabilities to sustain their operations beyond the buildout horizon. They also anticipated the importance of a smooth transition from developer to community control when the community was built out.

ABOVE Weston New Town became the city of Weston; **OPPOSITE** At Boca Raton, the Cloisters loggia reflects the area's heritage.

Key Points

- **AT RANCHO CALIFORNIA,** the strategic planning process led to the establishment of the water district in 1965, which had a long time horizon and adequate resources to serve both urban and agricultural needs well into the future. Thus, the full-service city of Temecula could successfully include both homes and businesses, while it was surrounded by viable agriculture and a famous wine district.

- **SCOTTSDALE—AND LATER FLORIDA'S BROWARD COUNTY,** the city of Boca Raton, the town of Longboat Key, and the city of Coral Gables—all used Cobb's master-planned communities as an effective strategy for more detailed implementation of their long-range city or countywide comprehensive plans. The master plans phased growth in coordination with school and civic facilities, and they balanced economic with residential growth.

- **COBB'S EARLY COMMUNITIES** made use of the "horizontal development" approach—whereby an organization focuses on master planning and bringing infrastructure, urban services, and high-quality community amenities to large tracts of land and makes them available to qualified residential, retail, or industrial project developers, who carry out the vertical development, that is, the homes and other buildings. Government jurisdictions saw that this practice added an important layer of private sector participation in infrastructure planning and building, quality control, coordination, marketing, public communication, and implementation to accomplish their comprehensive plan objectives.

- **MORE COMPACT, BETTER-ORGANIZED GROWTH**—as compared to unplanned sprawl—was fostered by the use of distinct residential villages in all of Cobb's communities. The villages were defined by open space and roadways as well as landscape elements, and they incorporated varied housing types and densities. Most villages included recreational amenities, which were completed before the homes went on the market. Some had schools and parks within their limits or directly adjacent. Walkability and biking were enhanced by the juxtaposition of compact development and open space along the grade-separated pathways of Camelback Walk at McCormick Ranch.

- **THE FORMATION OF FINANCIALLY VIABLE** utility and urban services districts, homeowners and community associations, and club organizations in all of Cobb's communities allowed a smooth transition to local governance after buildout. In 2011, the Cobb communities all operate as new cities, as part of existing cities or towns, or as unincorporated county communities, each with its own distinct governance structure.

- **THE INFRASTRUCTURE AND AMENITIES** in Cobb's communities were planned to accommodate future changes and adaptation over time. When the Rancho California Water District was formed in the 1960s, for example, near-term demand required only 12-inch water mains. The district, however, looked ahead to the future buildout, and it installed 36-inch mains, which avoided any risk of scarce supplies and high reconstruction or expansion costs in recent years.

PROTECT LOCAL HERITAGE—AND PROFITABILITY

In the 1960s, many communities' historic sites and buildings were viewed not as landmarks that gave them character but as outdated nuisances to be remodeled out of existence or torn down for something new. At that time, only a handful of U.S. communities, such as Charleston, South Carolina, and Savannah, Georgia, recognized the value of their historic districts and, therefore, enacted regulations to protect those landmark properties. In most outlying, rapidly growing areas, they were particularly at risk if they occupied a prominent location that would support a "higher and better use."

With a more comprehensive and longer-term perspective, Cobb and his team recognized that the protection of a community's unique character was not only the right thing to do, but also that it could be highly profit-

able. In areas experiencing rapid suburban development in the mid- to late-20th century, landmark buildings and original landscapes provided a marketable community identity that could not be created anew. For Cobb's team, therefore, incorporating elements of these original buildings and landscapes into the community provided immediately recognizable and distinctive features. Then with the addition of new developments, landscapes, and recreational facilities that were harmonious with this heritage, they could command a premium for both residential and commercial properties.

In Florida, where the Great Depression and devastating hurricanes had ended the ambitious and well-planned new communities of visionary developers Addison Mizner at Boca Raton, George Merrick at Coral Gables, and circus magnate and developer John Ringling at Longboat Key, Cobb maximized the value of landmarks and landscapes. These developers had selected some of the finest locations in Florida for their developments, and Cobb knew that protecting and incorporating elements of their original designs, well-planned roadways, and mature landscaping into his new plans offered greater value both immediately and over the long term.

These visionary early-20th-century developers had created concepts of resort communities that blended Mediterranean-influenced architecture and adapted to Florida lifestyles with robust public realms of landscaped streets, elaborate entries, golf courses, and civic elements to create a strong sense of place. With the widespread introduction of central air conditioning in the 1950s and 1960s, and subsequent population growth in the state of Florida, Cobb knew that these communities could be more than the seasonal resorts envisioned by their original 1920s developers. They could become year-round communities with substantial resort amenities that would be difficult to duplicate in less-favored locations. Of equal importance, Cobb saw the value of expanding these much-loved elements into the master-planned communities he was developing. Cobb also knew that original 1920s resort hotels and other iconic buildings could be restored and upgraded to bring greater luster to the community and create a favorable halo effect for his newly developing areas.

LEFT Cocoplum completed the historic Merrick Coral Gables master plan by including a yacht harbor on the main waterway and a series of islands served by a landscaped boulevard with traffic circles; OPPOSITE The Rancho California plan included Old Town Temecula, which has been revitalized.

Working carefully with the existing portions of Boca Raton, Coral Gables, and Longboat Key, Cobb's team of planners and developers carried forth—and brought to completion—the unique communities that had originated in the 1920s but were only completed in the late 20th century. In many ways, the protection and enhancement of existing community character was a precursor to the principles of new urbanism that came decades later.

Key Points

- **AT BOCA RATON,** Addison Mizner wanted to build the "greatest resort in the world," and in 1925, he completed magnificent tree-lined boulevards and constructed the first elements of the Boca Raton Hotel—the exclusive Cloister Inn and beach clubs. The following year, a powerful hurricane damaged the Florida Gold Coast, including Boca Raton,

Mizner's development company went bankrupt, and development came to a halt. When Chuck Cobb took over the new Arvida in 1972, he saw that Boca Raton was the special place that Mizner had envisioned and believed Mizner's goals could be achieved on the 5,000 acres that were still undeveloped in and adjacent to the city. By protecting the community's historic heart around the hotel and its unique landscapes and by blending the new areas and clubs with the existing features, Cobb and his team were able to expand upon that special place and make it part of all the residents' experience throughout Boca Raton— and a hugely profitable enterprise.

- **THE DEVELOPMENT OF CORAL GABLES,** an independent city southwest of downtown Miami, had followed George Merrick's 1920s plan after the Great Depression and World War II, and it became one of America's finest garden cities and one of the metropolitan area's pre-

mier residential and commercial districts. When Chuck Cobb gained control of the city's largest remaining undeveloped waterfront property in 1979, his team saw Merrick's original plan had called for—but never accomplished—a series of waterways and islands, and a boat harbor to complete the connection of the city to the bay. The Islands of Cocoplum that Cobb developed not only carried forward the garden city character of the rest of Coral Gables, but also created a boat harbor on the Coral Gables Waterway and a series of residential islands and waterways with mangrove preserves, thereby fulfilling Merrick's original plan and achieving a profitable venture.

ABOVE The Boca Raton Hotel and Club incorporated the original Mizner Cloisters Hotel; OPPOSITE Major commercial development in Weston.

- **ON LONGBOAT KEY** near Sarasota on Florida's west coast, circus magnate and real estate developer John Ringling planned a resort community and built the foundation of a Ritz-Carlton Hotel that was left unfinished because of the collapse of the Florida land boom, quickly followed by the Great Depression. More than three decades later, Chuck Cobb and Arvida realized the subsequent haphazard development on the key did not maximize the potential that Ringling had recognized for this ten-mile-long island of pure white quartz sand beaches. Gaining control of 1,100 acres on the southern third of the island where Ringling intended to build his resort, Cobb planned and developed two coordinated adjacent villages that transformed this part of the island into a desirable recreational and resort community. Adjacent to Ringling's intended hotel site, Cobb created a premier beachfront hotel and a town plaza with civic, shopping, and community institutions, setting new standards for the entire key and completing a successful venture.

- **AT SAWGRASS, FLORIDA,** Cobb saw the unrealized potential that the Jacksonville metropolitan area offered for beach and golf communities in its southeast sector in rural St. Johns County. In the 1930s, the Stockton family opened the historic Ponte Vedra Beach Club resort, but the lack of good access to Jacksonville and the dismal economic conditions of the Great Depression had hindered their progress. In 1977, with new freeway access under construction directly from central Jacksonville, Cobb was able to acquire the remaining land from the developer's family and created the Sawgrass Country Club. With an approach similar to those used at Boca Raton and Longboat Key, he expanded the golf and tennis club with first-class facilities, created a new beach club, and built a variety of housing. Pioneering the use of a prominent sports event to showcase a location, Cobb acquired additional lands and invited the Tournament Players Club to create a site in Sawgrass for its national golf tournament. The televised and print-reported events provided invaluable free publicity for the country club and for-sale homes, thereby realizing the potential begun in the 1930s of a celebrated new residential area for the region.

- **COBB APPLIED HIS PRINCIPLE** of protecting a community's cultural heritage in various other developments. He saw the potential at the Telluride Ski and Golf Resort in Colorado where the historic mining town had been safeguarded as a National Historic Landmark District since 1964. The resort attracted enough visitors to support significant investment in the historic buildings, which were adapted to current uses such as shops, restaurants, and inns. Cobb joined with Ron Allred, the developer of the Mountain Village at Telluride, to create a year-round ski and golf resort. In developing the Durango Mountain Ski Resort in Colorado, Cobb created an alpine community in the tradition of the small Colorado resort towns of La Plata and San Juan counties. At the Kirkwood Mountain Resort, he preserved elements of the 1864 Kirkwood Inn when it was rebuilt near the historic Mormon Emigrant Trail. And at the Tubac Golf Resort and Spa south of Tucson, Allred and the Tubac shareholders restored the 18th-century home of the Otero

Ranch landowners as a conference center and connected the resort through the San Juan Bautista National Historic Trail to Tubac, the first European settlement in Arizona.

- **COBB'S VISION HAS EXTENDED** his master-planning approach beyond just residential communities. At the University of Miami, where Cobb has served as a trustee, the chairman of the board, and the chairman of the master planning committee, his efforts enabled the last two presidents of the school to fulfill the original vision of George Merrick, "to establish Coral Gables as the educational center of the South." The plans that were designed by SWA Group and developed under Cobb's guidance gave the Coral Gables campus a distinctive south Florida identity appropriate to the largest private university in the southeast. The strategic plan, which was prepared when Cobb was chairman of the master planning committee, followed an overriding principle to establish an identity for the campus and to accommodate future growth on a truly walkable college campus environment that reflects its semi-tropical south Florida location. This principle was used, first, to swiftly minimize the asphalt parking and vehicle circulation that defaced the heart of the campus; then, to transform that central portion of the campus into a "tropical garden" of palms, plazas, fountains, and lawns that became a vehicle-free pedestrian precinct; and finally, to set landscape standards for any new development. Cobb carried out this plan as a trustee of the university.

- **COBB'S MASTER-PLANNING EFFORTS** also helped the Plymouth Congregational Church in the old Coconut Grove section of Miami preserve a historic church financed in 1917 by George Merrick, the developer of Coral Gables whose father had been a minister of the church. Cobb assisted in planning for conversion of the church property, which was designated by the city of Miami as a Heritage Conservation District in 1983, into a planned pedestrian campus around a common green, reusing coral rock buildings and adding new facilities to harmonize with the historic sanctuary.

MASTER-PLANNED COMMUNITIES AS ECONOMIC ENGINES

One hallmark of Chuck Cobb's developments was their repeated success as economic engines that created jobs and boosted the tax base and economic vitality for a region, thus benefitting the larger community as well as Cobb's bottom line. In making the development of his master-planned communities into a profitable business, his business model was to establish efficient organizations that had expertise in all aspects of land use: residential, retail, resort, industrial, and amenities. Each sector was expected to contribute to the profit of a new development. The industrial and commercial real estate divisions created sophisticated national marketing efforts to attract industries that fit well into the character and demographics of the community. The retail divisions had extensive national retailer contacts (as well as local ones) so they could introduce proven new retailers into the communities.

An important task for the each development division was determining the right mix of uses for a community and the appropriate phasing to boost immediate development activities, generate long-term profits, and en-

hance the quality of life for early residents and commercial users. After the development divisions had determined that overall set of goals and Cobb had approved the plan, each team carried out its particular portion of the larger strategy. These coordinated actions not only benefited each Cobb community but also provided a competitive advantage over nearby developments.

To support the initial phased development actions, the company's areawide managers had the ability to make deals such as subsidizing the early, and less profitable, development of retail services like supermarkets to increase initial home sales. Such subsidies were not viewed as a loss but rather as an investment in generating initial residents and supporting commercial users. The accelerated overall growth in the master-planned community would have the effect of increasing future retail land values, and this recapture was set in the business pro forma. Desirable early industrial users also were provided with incentives that were later recaptured by escalating industrial land values in upcoming years. As master

BELOW Weston Town Center has a mix of retail, office, and residential uses; **OPPOSITE** The Tournament Players Club stadium course and headquarters provide a national attraction for Sawgrass.

developer, Cobb wanted to enter as many land markets as possible with the intent to build out quickly (hence more profitably) and to increase the overall portfolio value by offering homebuyers nearby retail and jobs and by giving retailers and industries nearby customers and employees.

Key Points

- **THE CITIES OF TEMECULA, CALIFORNIA,** and Weston, Florida, have highly diversified tax bases because of the national commercial and industrial marketing programs implemented for these master-planned communities.

- **THE CITY OF BOCA RATON** annexed the Arvida Town Center and adjacent Via Verde Villages developed by Arvida in Palm Beach County to increase its tax base and help balance its budgets. The good reputation and early economic success of the Cobb communities facilitated annexations that not only benefited the annexed lands by becoming part of the well-known city but also reinforced their value as proven economic assets.

- **LONGBOAT KEY, FLORIDA,** gained a viable town center and job- and tax-generating visitor economy with the development of the Longboat Key Club. Recent policies of the town, however, have curtailed visitor use of its facilities because residents prefer "keeping Longboat, Longboat." The result has been a falloff in the town's vitality and economic activity, leading to closed retail shops and businesses. Current plans for a $400 million redevelopment of the Islandside portion of the Longboat Key Club, including the Inn on the Beach, are being considered and could be beneficial to the long-term economy of the town

but are controversial among residents. The outcome of this debate will be an example of whether the economic engine of a destination resort will have the community support necessary to continue to do its job.

- **THE INTRODUCTION OF HIGH-IMAGE** golf and tennis to Sawgrass, Florida, created a national destination sports base for the community and surrounding St. Johns County. The televised tournaments and national golf and tennis headquarters at Sawgrass provided publicity for the resort that was much more far-reaching and effective than a standard real estate marketing program. This level of "dream" golf and tennis, moreover, boosted housing sales, attracted visitors who patronized shops and hotels, and accelerated the community's development.

- **IN TEMECULA AND WESTON,** the strong job base created a near jobs/housing balance in those communities that continues today. Weston, with a population of about 65,000 has 35,000 jobs, close to what would be considered its labor force size. The proximity of so many good jobs has given both communities a competitive edge in attracting residents who want to work close to home. Conversely, they have attracted additional companies that recognize that a workforce that lives near the job is usually more stable and productive.

- **SOMETIMES, A LARGE NUMBER OF JOBS** within a community is not entirely a good thing. In Boca Raton, the 90,000 jobs are a boon for the local tax base but are out of balance with an available work force of 40,000 city residents. As a result, thousands of workers must commute from surrounding communities, creating transportation and traffic issues.

- **AT BOCA RATON,** IBM opened the first major business facility in the community built on land sold to it by Arvida. This high-profile IBM facility, which was the birthplace of the personal computer, established a technology base for the region that attracted related industries to the adjacent 800-acre Arvida Park of Commerce. This influx of tech businesses created substantial value for Cobb's company, and these facilities attracted high-paid professionals to the community, thereby boosting initial home sales and maintaining high resale values.

- **COBB RECOGNIZED** that areas outside a master-planned community's urban core could become economic engines, although not as the traditional business park or retail center. At Rancho California, the area's agricultural heritage was maintained by providing small five- to 20-acre estates on which citrus and avocados could be grown by cooperatives that continue to prosper today. Land was originally set aside by the master plan for vineyard development, which has evolved into the Temecula wine country, a significant new agricultural region. Today with 35 wineries, it provides a variety of jobs and has become one of southern California's tourist attractions.

- **FINALLY, THE COBB RESORT COMMUNITIES,** particularly the mountain skiing and golf resorts, provide economic stimulus to the supporting nearby rural communities. The resorts provide year-round and seasonal jobs, support local businesses, and help with transportation infrastructure. Where U.S. Forest Service lands are involved, the provision of private funds to maintain or restore sensitive environments is considered positive in the multiuse goals of Forest Service stewardship of these lands.

CREATING PHYSICAL AND SOCIAL COMMUNITY

One of Chuck Cobb's most vital goals was to establish a sense of community at the very beginning of development. To create an immediate sense of a physical and social community required significant upfront investments in infrastructure, community facilities, clubs, and other amenities. Typically, expenditures in the millions were required before any return could be had from the development of the community.

Some of these essential upfront costs could be readily absorbed into the budgets for the marketing and sales programs. Others could be financed through community service districts or other private or quasi-public mechanisms that established infrastructure and services based on projected revenue streams from users. Whereas some of the upfront investments in amenities would be offset through the faster appreciation in land values that they created, other costs were to be regained later at community buildout through sales of the clubs themselves or of business entities that were created to manage or service the amenities. To do all of this, Cobb and his team evolved approaches for creating physical and social community that would transform nationwide business practices.

Following the tradition of high-image communities such as Coral Gables and Beverly Hills, the extensive use of landscape was programmed into all of Cobb's developments to produce an easily seen and enjoyed sense of place and identity for the community as a whole and for each village and commercial area. Because major features—landscaped roadways, golf courses, public parks, and nature preserves—were largely completed before properties went onto the market, homebuyers and commercial users recognized the sense of place from the very start.

ABOVE Boca Beach Club hotel and condominiums in foreground, main resort across Lake Boca Raton; **OPPOSITE** Natural and developed landscape at Sawgrass helps create neighborhood identity.

The use of landscape as the primary physical basis of the community had several important advantages. First, landscape elements were cost-effective ways to achieve an immediate effect for a large land area. Second, the continuity of the streetscapes, entries, waterways, parks, and other open spaces created a unified feeling throughout the community. Third, many features performed double duty, such as the lakes, wetlands, and waterways that were necessary for water management or to meet environmental regulations, thus enabling their costs to be spread among several budgets. The landscape approach took engineering and environmental requirements and made them into amenities that increased the value of homes and businesses.

In Weston, the required water management areas were made into waterway amenities for the moderately priced villages. At Sawgrass, marsh preservation offered handsome value-boosting forested backdrops for homes as well as wildlife refuges. Properly maintained landscaping, moreover, never becomes old or out-of-date. It only becomes more beautiful with time and becomes an essential part of a community's identity.

Landscape was not seen as merely a passive setting or pretty backdrop but became a vital place for peoples' activities. Walking trails or paved paseos were included in all the Cobb communities and connected homes to local schools, parks, and shopping. Shaded streets, trails, and open spaces encouraged walking within the villages, greater opportunities to meet neighbors, and pleasant places to hold community events. A 2010 survey of the top 20 master-planned communities by RCLCO shows the wisdom of the use of landscaping as a basic community structure. In surveyed communities, homebuyers rank their most popular amenities as walking trails, open space, and gathering places.

While these wide-ranging landscape elements created the physical infrastructure to support a sense of community, additional catalysts—ones that further encouraged social activity and interaction—were another essential leading-edge Cobb policy. One favorite feature was the strategic use of clubs to bring people together in a meaningful, pleasant, and immediate way. The clubs, which focused on facilities for golf, tennis,

swimming, fitness, and family and social events, went beyond traditional country club eligibility and exclusiveness. In Cobb's communities, all residents and local businesses were eligible to be members.

Cobb and his teams understood that new residents of his communities had different interests, varied family situations, diverse incomes, and differing expected use of club facilities. To encourage most residents to join the clubs, the memberships were layered so residents could choose unlimited golf, tennis, or other special activities; take tennis and swim memberships; or join just as a social member. In every category, the fees were set according to the amount, type, and time of use. If a resident wanted to play golf as a tennis or social member, he or she could pay extra for an available tee time, but in any case, everyone was treated as a member with privileges.

Another community-enhancing feature was the immediate organization of well-run and well-financed community districts and homeowners associations for the new residents. Such associations were carefully set up at the outset and served several important purposes. In addition to creating an identity for neighborhoods within the larger community and offering regular social networking opportunities for the residents, these associations provided important services and governance on a localized basis, thereby giving new residents an immediate say over some affairs in their new community and offering protection for property values for buyers whose

ABOVE Open space need not be passive but can bring people together as at Camelback Walk at the McCormick Ranch; **OPPOSITE** The Boca West Club is a center for many kinds of community activity.

homes usually represented their largest single asset. These associations and districts continue today to provide efficient community-directed services.

Key Points

- **COBB'S TEAM TRANSFORMED** large tracts of land that lacked an easily recognizable identity and sense of place into handsome communities that would attract residents and businesses. These cost-effective landscape solutions can help build sustainable communities today. At Boca West, the configuration of the golf courses, waterways, and street landscapes created a series of residential villages, each with its own identity. At McCormick Ranch, the extension of Scottsdale's Indian Bend Greenway into the ranch and the creation of the Camelback Walk throughout the property used landscape elements not only to create a

visual focus for the new community but also as an activity corridor to tie the ranch into the existing city landscape.

- **INFILL OR URBAN REDEVELOPMENT** is more complex than suburban greenfield development, but lessons learned from the Cobb communities about how landscape can create civility and place in the suburbs can apply to urban challenges as well. In many ways, the Cobb communities were pioneers of the early 21st-century concept of landscape urbanism. Professor Charles Waldheim, of the Harvard Graduate School of Design, a leading advocate of the landscape urbanism movement, states that landscape rather than architecture is more capable of organizing the city, enhancing the urban experience, enriching the overall quality of life, and creating long-term value. Buildings are essential to a city, but the streets and spaces between buildings—the public landscape—define a place.

- **ONE OF THE GREATEST REAL ESTATE OPPORTUNITIES** of the early 21st century is infill development in the inner suburbs, particularly those with a well-recognized desirable identity and existing or potential transit connections to a thriving nearby city. With proper landscape planning, higher-density new development can blend into these communities rather than clash with their existing character.

- **LANDSCAPE CAN SUPPORT THE SMART GROWTH** goal of mixed uses. Well-designed landscape buffers, consistent street treatments, highlighting of natural features, and landscaped plazas and greenways have enabled single-family and mid- or high-rise residential uses to be located relatively close to each other at McCormick Ranch. Landscaping also unifies different office and warehouse uses at the Arvida Park of Commerce, office and residential uses at Carillon, and retail and residential uses at Weston.

- **FROM THE VERY START,** a variety of clubs can create a sense of community through social interaction. Clubs also can produce immediate multiple revenue sources for the developer. In Boca Raton, the Boca West Club has accommodated as many as 8,000 members, and the Boca Raton Hotel and Club 4,000 members. The clubs were eventually sold at buildout through a purchase agreement between the members and the Cobb development entities.

- **CLUBS AND RESORT ACTIVITIES** at Cobb communities not only strengthened the sense of community and generated income for the developer, but they also drew revenue from visitors who were prospects for purchasing a home in the community.

- **THE USE OF CLUBS** to create an early sense of community was easily adaptable to fit different Cobb developments. The private, gated, exclusive communities of Fisher Island and Coto de Caza have private-ownership equity clubs for wealthy local residents. The clubs at Weston are open to all residents and appeal to a range of largely middle-class local families. In between, the clubs at Willow Springs and Cullasaja are family oriented, and for resident and guest use only, while the clubs at Boca Raton, Longboat Key, McCormick Ranch, and the ski resorts are used by residents and resort guests.

- **THE COBB COMMUNITIES** pioneered televised competitive sports events as a way to demonstrate the appeal of their recreation club facilities. Using the golf, tennis, or swim facilities at a number of community clubs, they attracted a national audience. These professional tournaments were followed by a rich variety of intramural sports events such as the "Challenge of the Villages," a series of competitions between the residential villages at Boca Raton.

- **THE USE OF MASTER HOMEOWNER** and community associations and districts such as the Boca West Master Association or the Indian Trace Community Development District at Weston offers lessons on ways to set up, control, and maintain the amenities, infrastructure, and development over time. They are cost-effective and efficient governance structures that respond to local control and ensure the quality and maintenance of the facilities that contribute to the communities' identity.

■ **COBB COMMUNITIES PROVIDED** soft infrastructure in the form of newsletters and bulletin boards and at Weston pioneered an online interactive community called "Town Talk" to provide information on events, schools, and clubs and activities at the Weston Community Center.

■ **IN COBB'S MASTER-PLANNED COMMUNITIES,** residents and businesses did more than *say* that they valued these places, they proved those statements with actions that affected the value of their homes and quality of day-to-day life. When residents of the 1,300-acre previously developed Bonaventure community voted for annexation to Weston, two-thirds of the voters approved the measure, indicating the high esteem its closest neighbors held for Weston.

PROVIDING EDUCATION AND HEALTH

To create a sense of community and attract families to buy homes, Chuck Cobb always planned for high-quality and conveniently located schools and active parks in his communities. These on-site schools and recreational facilities provided a substantial marketing advantage over standard subdivisions where the nearest schools might be miles away. At the Cobb developments, schools and recreational facilities were located where children could safely walk or bike to school and served as community centers where residents could interact with each other, feel a greater sense of belonging, and achieve a sense of community more quickly.

The promise of a healthy lifestyle was another foundation and marketing theme of Cobb's communities. Decades before health and fitness became a goal for many Americans, these wellness ideals were fostered in Cobb communities by a focus on outdoor recreation, either structured around golf, tennis, swimming, boating, fitness centers, and school playfields, or focused on hiking, bicycling, and walking trails. All the Cobb communities had sites appropriate for health care professionals' offices and health clinics and, in some cases, full-scale hospitals.

ABOVE The Cleveland Clinic of Florida at Weston; **OPPOSITE** Neighborhood school at Weston.

Key Points

- **AT RANCHO CALIFORNIA,** Cobb learned one of the most critical lessons: the importance of providing on-site modern schools for all residents from the opening day. When the first residents moved into their Rancho California homes in the late 1960s, not all of the schools had opened yet. At that time, developers relied on local school districts to serve these new pupils, but the fast growth often caused these districts to fall behind in providing adequate new facilities. Therefore, some of the Rancho California children in the higher grades had to travel long distances to a rural school district. Recognizing that this drawback was affecting home sales, Cobb began a more aggressive policy of assisting the districts in providing all grades of school in a timely manner by coordinating the process with residential construction.

- **COBB DID NOT ENTIRELY RELY ON** often overburdened or slow-moving districts to carry out school planning and construction on their own. In the remainder of Rancho California and in all subsequent Cobb communities, school and park sites were not only designated on the plan, but also the Cobb team worked closely with the various districts to ensure that schools were open and ready for the pupils in close conjunction with the phases of development. In some cases, Cobb donated the sites for schools. Other times, where the districts were unable to provide facilities in a timely manner, he assisted them in the financing or construction of the schools. These financial arrangements were leading-edge efforts to make education a top priority.

- **SCHOOLS WERE LOCATED CLOSE** to residential villages so that students could walk or bicycle to school, freeing their parents from long dropoff and pickup drives. At McCormick Ranch, Camelback Walk—which has pedestrian underpasses at major thoroughfares—offers students a safe, vehicle-free route to school. These routes also provide safe walking trails for adults and a unifying linear park knitting together the community.

- **COBB RECOGNIZED** that sports and fitness clubs and parks were only one part of offering residents a healthy lifestyle. Wherever possible, his team sought out major hospitals and medical facilities. Such efforts reaped major accomplishments, such as the Scottsdale Health Campus at McCormick Ranch and Weston's nationally prominent Cleveland Clinic. Such state-of-the-art facilities help maintain those communities' desirability and appeal to homeowners as they age. The young parents of the 1970s and 1980s, who were focused on their children's education, are now empty nesters who are concerned about their long-term health and wellness.

- **HIGHER EDUCATION** was not built into the new Cobb communities, but his companies provided support to nearby colleges and universities. Not only were these actions the right to thing to do in those locations where his company had a major presence, but the schools provided another lure for potential residents and for companies in the office and industrial parks. His company worked with the many technology companies in the Park of Commerce to promote and support engineering programs at Florida Atlantic University in Boca Raton.

PROTECTING OPEN SPACE, NATURAL LANDSCAPE, AND AGRICULTURAL RESOURCES

Since the 1960s, the preservation of active and passive open space has been an important principle in environmentally sustainable planning for areas experiencing rapid growth. The public's growing concern about the environment has encouraged additional government measures to protect environmentally sensitive lands. Although many builders fought such regulations, enlightened developers supported them, knowing that buyers willingly paid higher home prices in communities with protected open space. Protection of open space was the right thing to do and a profitable development strategy as well.

Cobb's communities have been at the forefront of measures to protect open space and have made a point to keep up with evolving regulatory requirements. His actions, moreover, encouraged other developers to take such steps, because he proved these features boosted the bottom line. In 1964, long before agricultural and environmental protection had gone mainstream, Rancho California's plan protected agricultural uses and environmentally sensitive lands from development. At Cocoplum and Longboat Key, Cobb's team embraced the mandated mangrove protection as a key component of the master plan to prevent shoreline erosion and protect habitat in Biscayne Bay. At Longboat Key, a wildlife preserve was cooperatively established with local environmental agencies at the Sarasota Bay shoreline to protect those mangrove areas. The Boca Beach Club used vegetated dunes rather than seawalls as shoreline protection. Weston and Sawgrass have substantial wetland preservation areas, and Weston has protected components of the regionwide Everglades Restoration Plan.

In Cobb's resort communities, a primary goal of the master plans is to protect environmentally sensitive lands and resources and to carefully harmonize the limited development areas with the natural character. The joint public/private planning processes for these specialized master-planned communities involve rural counties and, in many cases, the U.S. Forest Service for the mountain ski and golf resorts.

Key Points

- **PROTECTED AGRICULTURAL LANDS** can provide identity and economic advantages to a master-planned community. At Rancho California, agricultural land use was designated to provide a greenbelt around the urban areas that has been sustained for over five decades with cooperative farming of citrus and avocado orchards throughout the estate areas and large vineyard areas on the gently rolling hills above the city of Temecula. This popular, award-winning wine district provides direct and spinoff jobs. The steady flow of visitors they generate is supporting the city's plans to strengthen its long-dormant Old Town, which requires more than local residents to become a successful destination and job generator. Following Cobb's lead, Riverside County subsequently took steps to make the agricultural and open spaces that were set aside by the master plan into permanent preserves, by creating the Citrus and Vineyard Protection Policy Area and the Vail Lake, Equestrian Policy, and Santa Rosa Plateau protection zones, now covering an area of 27,500 acres.

- **NOT ALL COMMUNITIES RECOGNIZE** the synergy that can be created by protected farmland balanced with limited development. When Cobb tried to adapt this same combination of development and protected agriculture to a large master-planned community at Amberton in Ventura County in the 1970s, both environmental and local agricultural interests blocked any such approach. Here local small farmers tapped into a no-

BELOW The vineyard areas of Rancho California have created the Temecula wine district with 35 wineries; **OPPOSITE** Marsh preservation areas at Sawgrass.

growth sentiment that blocked a freeway extension, stopped a new state college campus, and prevented the proposed mixed housing and agricultural use development. Today, the Amberton area's small rural towns have been modestly expanded with housing and scattered large-lot residential development, while the majority of the proposed site retains small-scale agricultural uses. To this day, Ventura County has maintained an approach that might be considered "no growth" rather than "smart growth." Although residents had every right to shape their community's destiny, they lost many benefits of a well-done master-planned community, such as job creation, better educational facilities, and more opportunities for young people. This approach has to be weighed against overall community lifestyle goals and five decades of county policy on a case-by-case basis.

■ **OPEN SPACE AND NATURAL SYSTEMS** are the basis for the lifestyles in all of Chuck Cobb's communities, and their protection has been a community hallmark. Cobb's communities prove that setting aside large open-space areas is financially feasible and creates a more livable community with enduring long-term value. Today, residents generally support such environmental land use policies from their governments. After Weston became a city, it continued to emphasize the environment by acquiring an additional 4,000 acres of protected wetlands and Everglades restoration areas.

■ **COBB WAS A PIONEER** in recognizing that resort communities were good places to introduce new ways to protect natural and scenic resources, because the users of these places enjoy the natural settings and, therefore, appreciate strong measures for their protection.

■ **A VAST NUMBER OF ACRES** have been set aside as open space in Cobb's communities. Rancho California includes the 8,200-acre Santa Rosa Environmental Preserve and the 8,850-acre Vail Lake Open Space and Recreation Preserve; McCormick Ranch has its Indian Bend Wash greenways and Camelback Walk. Longboat Key and Cocoplum have hundreds of acres of mangrove and shoreline habitat preservation. Coto de Caza includes a 475-acre wilderness park with a heritage oak forest that reflects the history of this beautiful inland valley.

■ **IN THE COBB SKI AND MOUNTAIN RESORTS,** energy-efficiency and the visitors' experience are enhanced by the communities being planned within a compact area. The concentration and control of small development footprints, set carefully within these environmentally sensitive areas, ensures the goal of maximum protection and enjoyment of the natural resources, as well as a more pedestrian-oriented lifestyle. Durango Mountain Village, built on 600 acres of private land with stewardship responsibilities for recreational use of 2,500 acres of U.S. Forest Service land, received the National Ski Areas Association Silver Eagle award in 2010 for excellence in fish and wildlife habitat protection.

■ **GOLF IS A PRIMARY AMENITY** in Cobb's communities. In many cases, multiple courses were used to satisfy the recreational needs of the communities. Golf played multiple roles, first as an attractive open space for the entire community. The plans ensured the golf courses had "windows" that displayed visual open space for all to enjoy. Second, golf was a key asset for the clubs, playing an important role in creating a sense of community. Third, golf was a key marketing ingredient in gaining recognition for the community, and finally golf was a high-amenity setting for homes, and even businesses, and garnered a premium for real estate.

HOUSING AFFORDABILITY

When Rancho California broke ground in 1964 and when construction started at Weston in 1980, both communities were planned to include affordable housing relative to their respective markets. From the start, both communities included a mix of single-family houses, townhouses, and condominiums. These communities could offer affordable prices compared to older, closer-in neighborhoods because of their lower land costs. From a marketing standpoint, the high-quality amenities and open space offset smaller-than-customary lot sizes, allowing the communities to compete with large-lot, stand-alone subdivision housing. The inclusion of the townhomes and condominiums at Rancho California and Weston enabled smaller households, such as just-married couples or seniors, to live in and enjoy the benefits of the planned communities. This wider diversity of housing types and prices served Cobb's interest, because it spread the risk by broadening the pool of potential buyers.

LEFT The Boca Beach Club dunes are protected by vegetation; OPPOSITE Mixed housing types at Boca West.

Cobb planned to serve the upper third of the housing market, as was appropriate for highly amenitized communities. His developments would be competitive with large-lot, upscale subdivisions and desirable inner-suburban communities. When Weston began development in the early 1980s, it offered homes at very affordable prices, most likely serving more than the upper third of the market. In 2006 when it had a much higher median housing price than Broward County as a whole, *Business Week* still named it "one of the best affordable suburbs in the U.S."

Even given the targeting of upper portions of the housing market, Cobb's commitment to offer a variety of housing types and prices was a pioneering step at the time. Many jurisdictions and their residents, however, did not see this variety as a benefit. At Boca Raton and Coral Gables, Cobb had planned to provide a mix of housing types and prices but encountered inflexible opposition. A group of residents in a referendum and then the city of Boca Raton in its comprehensive plan prevented any significant multifamily housing. At Cocoplum, the city of Coral Gables prevented a residential mix that included relatively affordable homes in small-lot clusters.

The emphasis by Boca Raton and Cocoplum on large lots and large single-family homes was common. Throughout the 1970s, 1980s, and 1990s, Cobb repeatedly encountered jurisdictions and local residents that hampered the creation of genuine master-planned communities with a mixture of housing prices and types. Whether because of a desire to keep out renters and more modest-income residents or a desire to increase property values for existing neighborhoods, the trends were almost universal in those times. Single-family homes were the most favored housing type, and those who could afford them tended to keep other kinds of housing out.

Key Points

■ **ALTHOUGH SEEMINGLY COUNTERINTUITIVE,** large single-family homes typically sold faster and at higher profit margins than higher-density alternatives. A major reason was the overwhelming predominance in the suburban housing market of middle- and upper-middle-class nuclear families with children who preferred—and could afford—single-family houses. At the time, some experts believed that real estate trend was unending, and many builders specialized in ever-larger houses to appeal to such families. The market's near obsession with traditional nuclear families and single-family homes of larger and larger

size and the notion that attached units would bring "undesirables" or reduce property values narrowed affordable housing opportunities.

■ **THE OVERRELIANCE** of most suburban development on large-lot single-family houses may put such properties at risk as housing markets change over time. In the late 20th and early 21st centuries, the nation began to experience significant demographic changes. Today unmarried adults are more common than married ones, and the overwhelming majority of households consist of single adults or couples without children. Families are having fewer children than in the previous generation, and families with children represent only about 25 percent of households. Likewise, suburbs have become job generators, and workers of all economic classes, ethnic groups, social status, and family type come to fill those jobs. The suburbs have become more than just bedroom communities for one dominant type of family. Given this change in family types and structure, a dramatic shift in the kinds, costs, and sizes of housing in master-planned communities would be expected to occur. However, a 2009 RCLCO survey shows that 90 percent of

homebuyers in master-planned communities still favored single-family houses, although lot and house sizes are shrinking. Apparently, some of today's communities are repeating the mistakes that were made in the 1980s and 1990s by not offering a broader mix of housing types and potentially greater affordability.

- **ANOTHER FACTOR** that affected affordability was the premium that developed in all categories of homes in master-planned communities because of the growing perception of the real added value of this type of community. Even in economic downturns when the overall housing market suffered, homes in master-planned communities sold better and held their value better than subdivision housing. A key example was the severely depressed housing market during the 1980s when master-planned communities in Houston held their value as adjacent subdivisions were foreclosed and boarded up. The effects of the housing collapse triggered by the recession of 2008 are still being played out, and time will tell what consequences this potential structural change in the housing market will bring.

- **SOME OF THE COBB COMMUNITIES,** such as Fisher Island and Coto de Caza, by virtue of their special locations and natural features were planned as upscale lifestyle developments targeted for the upper 5 to 10 percent of the housing market. They became successful because of the Cobb teams' expertise in high-end private equity clubs.

- **COBB'S RESORT COMMUNITIES,** such as Durango and Kirkwood, pursued different objectives for housing. Although these communities are primarily family-oriented second-home communities, they always in-cluded properties and services for substantial visitor use. Local jurisdictions and owners in these resort communities usually had no issues with condominium units or higher density, which were handled in the master plans by creating separate neighborhoods of compatible types of units, such as a mix of single-family houses and townhouses, or condominiums and lodges. Cobb was one of the first developers to address the issue of affordability of vacation homes in a well-planned and protected natural environment. He made use of small units, fractional ownership units, and a sophisticated system of marketing and managing condominium rentals to generate revenues and help ameliorate costs. These opportunities for families have been successfully accomplished at Durango, Kirkwood, and the Walt Disney Resorts.

- **BY TARGETING THE UPPER THIRD** of the housing market, the Cobb communities obviously would not provide affordability in the larger sense. However, this strategy was a reasonable business decision given housing policies of the local jurisdictions of that time and was consistent with the suburban marketplace of the 20th century that relied on trickle-down and urban sprawl to serve the middle and lower parts of the market.

- **TODAY,** because of changing public housing policies, primary-home master-planned communities have in some cases been required to use inclusionary zoning or subsidies to provide a greater range of affordability than was possible by relying on just the housing marketplace. This step toward creating affordability may be effective if density restrictions are relaxed to help ameliorate the costs of these kinds of units.

TRANSPORTATION AND LAND USE

When Charles Cobb developed his master-planned communities, it was the era of automobile-focused suburban growth serving two-parent families with children. The automobile represented comfortable and quick personal transportation on the still-uncrowded new roadways at a time of inexpensive gasoline. This flexible capacity to move people and goods around the nation also led to the development of shopping centers and low-density employment centers.

The automobile industry was a cornerstone of the American economy, and government at all levels supported low-density growth. At the federal level, the policies were directed toward low gasoline prices and housing finance policies that encouraged low-density single-family homes. At the federal and state levels, highways were generously funded and maintained, and at the local level, zoning favored low-density housing and ample free parking in shopping and business areas. Transit seemed necessary only as a minor adjunct for the handicapped or service workers who could not afford cars.

Transportation needs and use are closely related to land use densities and mixes of uses. Where local jurisdictions and markets favor low-density and ample free parking, parking becomes the basic determinant of land use density and mix and the key to transportation options and feasibilities. The large areas of parking typically required by local jurisdictions have the effect of dramatically lowering the density of all development. The significant areas of land dedicated to surface parking create a coarser mix of land uses that inhibit walkability. The Cobb communities therefore not only lacked transit support from the region or metropolitan area but also were required to be built at densities and mixes of uses that made providing alternatives to the automobile difficult to accomplish and uneconomical for either private developers or public agencies.

OPPOSITE Single-family homes at Millpond Village in Boca Raton; BELOW Bicycle lanes at McCormick Ranch.

Only a generation after the development of the Cobb communities did any significant federal, state, or regional planning policies emerge that encouraged modes of transportation other than the automobile. Bringing more sustainable transportation modes to Cobb's communities has been made easier by the original planning framework that carefully located jobs, housing, shopping, schools, and recreation proximately, and by the several-decades-old villages, town centers, and pedestrian and bicycle systems that can be upgraded to meet current standards.

A walkable main street in Weston.

Key Points

- **COBB'S COMMUNITIES WERE PLANNED** around the car as the means of transportation because the era dictated it. The development of many communities was coordinated with the opening of nearby Interstate highways. Freeway exits not only determined local transportation patterns, but they also affected the overall planning for the community, such as which uses were located where on the property.

- **IN PLANNING COBB'S COMMUNITIES,** his team looked beyond the era's practice of laying out roadways solely to move as many cars as quickly as possible through the community. They recognized that roadways could include pedestrian walkways and bicycle paths. A community's road systems were carefully planned in a hierarchy that allowed the neighborhood and village streets to be designed for slower traffic with narrow vehicle ways and a strong pedestrian character like the "public garden" approach in Cocoplum. In laying out necessary arterials, Cobb and his team included pedestrian and bicycle systems that were separated from the vehicle lanes, as at McCormick Ranch. They minimized negative traffic impacts from major roadways to nearby residential areas with landscaped berms and walls at Boca Raton. To make wide roadways more attractive, they provided landscaped medians and curbside planting strips, marking the first time in Florida that private landscape was added to state roads. At Willow Springs and Sawgrass, they preserved native forest along the edges of roadways.

- **COBB AND HIS TEAM** foresaw that traffic was going to increase as each community achieved buildout and nearby areas beyond the property were fully developed. Like nearly everyone else, they did not, however, realize that automobile ownership and vehicle miles traveled were going to increase exponentially, far beyond the increase in population. This trend resulted from the multiplier effect of people traveling greater distances and more vehicular trips replacing trips by walking or bicycling. A prime example was driving children to neighborhood schools and parks or to sports practices and games, whereas in earlier times, young people had walked or biked to such destinations.

- **BECAUSE LOCAL OR REGIONAL** public transit service was unavailable or insufficiently provided in Cobb's communities, some attempts were made to plan for private community shuttles to serve people without cars. These proved difficult because of the high costs for the few riders served and were sustainable only in the resort communities. Shuttles

at the resorts were subsidized to provide access for visitors and employees, and thereby could serve some residents. The pink buses and water taxi of the Boca Hotel, the ski buses and shuttles to the airports at the mountain resorts, the gondola at Telluride, and the water taxis and shuttles at Walt Disney World are examples.

- **RANCHO CALIFORNIA,** Temecula, Boca Raton, Weston, Longboat Key, and McCormick Ranch are still automobile-oriented today, even as they have added limited bus, shuttle, or trolley service. They are still waiting for regional transit alternatives that must be launched on a metropolitan area–wide basis to provide viable transportation choices. Some of these new transit options only entered the planning process in the early 21st century, such as the Temecula-Murrieta station on the proposed statewide California high-speed-rail project and the accompanying local bus transit terminal, or the expanded Tri-Rail station and shuttle services at the Arvida Park of Commerce in Boca Raton.

- **THE MOST POTENT TOOL** for providing better use of transportation resources was the original master plan for each community, which placed various destinations in proximity even though the densities were low and the mix of uses relatively coarse. Studies show between 25 and 50 percent of residents' total trips are made *within* most mas-

ter-planned communities rather than beyond their limits, which saves time behind the wheel and automotive costs.

- **THE BALANCED LAND USE MIX** that is the hallmark of most Cobb communities has been receptive to the dramatic changes in local policies in the early 21st century. At Temecula (Rancho California) and Weston, the most recent developments afford a finer-grained, transit-friendly density and more walkable villages such as Harveston in Temecula, the mixed-use Main Street of Weston Town Center, or the new "lifestyle" addition to the Town Center at Boca Raton.

ABOVE Boats replace automotive transportation at Disney World; **OPPOSITE** McCormick Ranch was designed to connect to Scottsdale and has become an infill development to the city.

- **SHIFTING FROM AUTOMOBILE-ORIENTED MODELS** to alternative modes of transportation offers huge potential for smarter redevelopment using the large land areas currently occupied by so much surface parking. With support of the jurisdictions, these parking lots can be redeveloped for structured parking, higher land use densities, and a finer grain mix of uses. Changing surface parking lots to built uses not only increases overall density to support transit but also transforms the dead street space used for car storage into continuous activity, thereby enhancing walkability.

■ **AT THE TEMECULA-MURRIETA STATION** at Rancho California, planning has entered the early stages for a mixed-use transit-oriented development adjacent to the proposed high-speed-rail station and bus terminal. Transit-oriented developments are a creative way to retrofit the new transit infrastructure into existing communities.

In the 1960s and 1970s, Cobb's communities coordinated their development with the new interstate highway infrastructure. At Rancho California, Cobb donated a significant portion of the land for I-15, which made his property more accessible and valuable. At Weston and Boca Raton, his company provided right-of-way for I-75 and early financing and enhancements of freeway interchanges. Future communities could follow these precedents by having new transit planned and financed with basic government support and then partly subsidized by private real estate development like the transit-oriented developments at the station areas. This approach to public/private coordinated planning and financing of transit-oriented development could be extended throughout the master-planned community with feeder light rail or public bus systems or by private shuttles or car-sharing enterprises, serving higher-density transit-friendly land uses.

A BETTER WAY FOR GREENFIELD DEVELOPMENT

Although the advocates of smart growth principles promote infill ventures for urban and suburban growth, greenfield development has been the overwhelming model throughout the United States from the 1950s to the present. Today, although infill growth represents an increasing percentage of new housing in some metropolitan areas, the U.S. Environmental Protection Agency estimates that the great majority of new growth will continue to occur on outlying greenfields for the foreseeable future.

Given this inexorable trend, the key question becomes: What is the best way to carry out greenfield development? To formulate the most effective and practical policies, more focused questions must be asked:

■ **WHERE SHOULD SUCH GROWTH BE ALLOWED** to protect natural environments?

■ **WHERE SHOULD NEW DEVELOPMENT BE LOCATED,** while including different types of uses, to minimize costly, time- and energy-consuming trips between homes, work, shopping, and schools?

■ **WHERE SHOULD DEVELOPMENT BE LOCATED** to minimize first-time infrastructure costs and long-term maintenance?

■ **HOW CAN A GREATER SENSE OF COMMUNITY** and interaction be encouraged among all residents?

Chuck Cobb recognized many of these issues long before many developers or jurisdictions. McCormick Ranch, although technically a greenfield development at the edge of Scottsdale, was connected to the city's roadways, greenways, and civic infrastructure, and it became a part of the city as other growth spread beyond the ranch in subsequent years. After McCormick Ranch's success, Scottsdale relied on master-planned communities as a growth management mechanism to raise development standards and provide privately financed infrastructure.

At Boca Raton, much of Arvida's 5,000 acres were greenfields either within the city limits or directly adjacent to the city boundaries in Palm Beach County. However, in both jurisdictions a few scattered subdivisions and commercial sites broke the Arvida lands into multiple parcels. The Cobb strategy was to plan the lands as a unified whole with uses that harmonized with adjacent built parcels. The result was a highly unified land use mix that filled out the city and led to the eventual annexation of almost all the county lands into the city. This was smart growth for the city of Boca Raton.

In the 1970s, Weston was a large greenfield parcel at the Everglades edge of Broward County. Because chaotic suburban sprawl was moving up Florida's Gold Coast toward Weston, Chuck Cobb and the county planned the site's development together following the state-mandated planning process as a Development of Regional Impact. They created a master-planned community that became a full-service city, with a town center, job centers, diverse housing, and amenities. The city of Weston's 2009 Comprehensive Plan validates this public/private Greenfield effort: "As a planned community, with a defined footprint and density, the city will not contribute to the sprawl and continued expansion of utilities that has become a prominent development concern across the nation. The city is nearly built out, and as such, nearly all future projects will be redevelopment projects with existing infrastructure available."

OPPOSITE The Arvida Park of Commerce was developed as part of the city of Boca Raton.

The communities at Longboat Key and Cocoplum were in fact large infill developments within partly developed cities. Sawgrass was a large greenfield property at the edge of the Jacksonville metropolitan area, and it was transformed into a master-planned community that created substantial jobs and economic activity and added a nationally significant golfing and sports center to the area. More recent phases of the Cobb communities, such as the walkable Village of Harveston at Rancho California and a main street–oriented town center at Weston, incorporate more current thinking that favors walking over driving and energy-efficient green building to reduce carbon emissions and give residents more lifestyle options.

By 2010, more than 400 master-planned communities were under development in the United States—mostly in greenfield locations. A review by the real estate consulting firm RCLCO indicates that the most successful ones are well established primary-home communities that contain or are near job centers and that offer a wide range of housing choices with amenities in place. The study notes the most important factor to homebuyers is the quality of schools and the most important amenities are walking trails, open spaces, town centers, and gathering places.

CONCLUSION

Cobb's communities display many of the characteristics of the best current development practices and pioneered many of their standards. Standing the test of time, they are examples of mid-to-late-20th-century models that work economically and environmentally and substantially meet the smart growth principles. These communities represented smart growth principles well before the term originated. Because of their well-chosen locations, careful plans, and amenities, they remain highly desirable communities and continue to evolve toward current smart growth and sustainability standards. They provide lessons for today's developers with their proven strategies of using public/private planning; protecting local heritage; creating jobs and economic growth; evolving community through clubs, associations, and complete landscape urbanism; enhancing education and health of their residents; and protecting agriculture and environmentally sensitive areas. They also offer lessons on the continued difficulties of providing affordable housing, transportation choices and transit-oriented densities, and land use mixes, given the conflicting priorities of American development policies as they interact with a market-driven development framework. Finally, they offer proven ways to better shape and control the large segment of greenfield development that will be necessary in the coming decades.

Biography of Charles E. Cobb

Over his long career, Chuck Cobb guided the development of numerous smart growth master-planned communities and other projects. In addition to his real estate endeavors, Cobb has distinguished himself as a corporate chief executive officer, investment professional, naval officer, athlete, ambassador, and civic activist. Cobb was born on May 9, 1936, in Fresno, California. His great-grandfather had traveled from Indiana in a covered wagon to Fresno in the Central Valley of California in 1868. The Cobb pioneers traveled over the Sierra Nevada mountains on the Mormon Emigrant Trail through what is now Cobb's Kirkwood Resort south of Lake Tahoe, which is described in this book.

In Cobb's early years in Fresno, he was an outstanding athlete who played football and basketball and ran track as one of the nation's best high hurdlers. Later at Stanford University and then as an officer in the U.S. Navy, he became the fifth-best high hurdler in the world and was the alternate on the 1960 U.S. Olympic team. Cobb attended the Stanford Graduate School of Business where he received his MBA in finance and general management. During this time, he played first-string wing on Stanford's rugby team, which was one of the best in the nation.

EARLY CAREER

After receiving his MBA, Cobb worked for the investment management firm of Dodge and Cox and later became the chief financial officer of Kaiser Aluminum's real estate subsidiaries. While still in his 20s, Cobb led the efforts to finance Kaiser's purchase of the 95,000-acre Rancho California in 1964. In 1967, at the age of 30, he became president of this master-planned community, as well as president of the City Management Company, one of Kaiser's subsidiaries, where he oversaw development of a regional shopping center, office, and apartment complex in Orange County, California. Rancho California, the McCormick Ranch in Scottsdale, and Amberton in Ventura County are included in this book. All owned by Kaiser and its partner Aetna Life Insurance Company, the communities were Cobb's responsibility from 1967 to 1971.

In 1971, Cobb was offered the position of CEO of Arvida, which was then a relatively small real estate company with revenues of less than $5 million. During the next decade, Cobb and his team built Arvida into the nation's largest community development company. In the late 1970s, Penn Central, the reorganized former railroad, purchased 100 percent of the then publicly held Arvida. The many impressive master-planned communities built by Arvida under Cobb are included in this book.

In 1980, after Penn Central purchased 100 percent of Arvida, Cobb was asked to be a group executive in charge of its real estate, resort, and leisure subsidiaries, which included Arvida Corporation and Six Flags amusement parks, among other properties. Two years later, in 1982, Cobb was asked to be the chief operating officer (COO) of Penn Central and in charge of all the company's approximately 100 businesses and about 40,000 employees.

In 1983, the Penn Central board decided to again make Arvida a publicly held company by selling 75 percent to the public and retaining 25 percent. Cobb agreed to retire from the position as COO of Penn Central and to continue his role as a director of Penn Central along with being the CEO of Arvida. He agreed to help Penn Central sell Six Flags and some of its other businesses.

PURCHASE OF ARVIDA

After Six Flags was sold to Bally Industries, Equitable Life Insurance Company made an offer to purchase 100 percent of Arvida for approximately $300 million. Cobb was only told of Equitable's offer 24 hours before the Penn Central board was to meet to approve it. (Because Cobb was a director of Penn Central, the board was required by law to give him the 24-hour notice.) Many of the Penn Central board members were concerned Cobb would try to arrange a competing offer, which might confuse the Equitable Life negotiations, but they were very confident he could not finance a $300 million purchase offer within this short time after being notified.

When Cobb received the notice at 5 p.m. one night in October 1983 that Equitable had made the offer, he knew he needed to move fast because he had only 24 hours to arrange a competitive offer. The board of Penn Central would vote on this sale at 5 p.m. the next afternoon. His first call was to his friend Richard Rainwater, who was the top investment officer of the Bass Brothers in Fort Worth, Texas. A few months earlier, Cobb had presented the opportunity for the Bass Brothers to buy

Six Flags from Penn Central, and Rainwater had said that he and the Bass Brothers would be interested in buying Six Flags if Cobb would agree to be the CEO and invest his entire net worth in the company. Cobb did not have the same confidence in Six Flags that he had in Arvida, so he passed on the Six Flags offer. Now he called Rainwater to partner in the purchase of Arvida, this time prepared to put his entire net worth into his share of the purchase price.

Because Rainwater could not meet until 10 that night, Cobb chartered an airplane to meet with him that night at a Fort Worth restaurant. As Cobb was running out of the office, he saw John Temple and Frank Zohn and told them that they needed to go with him and to bring all the financial statements from the previous years and the appraisals on all of Arvida's properties.

When Cobb, Temple, and Zohn met with Rainwater at 10 p.m., Rainwater said it was too late at night to read all the financial statements and appraisals. However, he proposed that the group offer to pay slightly more than the approximately $300 million offer from Equitable, making at least a $2 million nonrefundable hard deposit with no contingencies. He proposed $1 million of the deposit come from Cobb, Temple, and Zohn and the other $1 million from the Bass Brothers. He warned the three that the Bass Brothers frequently walked away from million-dollar deposits or option payments and that they had to recognize that their $1 million was totally at risk with a very good chance they would lose it if the Bass Brothers decided after reading the material they did not want to make the investment.

By 2 a.m., the Bass Brothers' attorneys had drafted a purchase contract and had a bank prepare a $2 million cashier's check. Because Cobb, Temple, and Zohn did not have $1 million in cash with them (and, in fact, did not have that much cash in their combined bank accounts), the Bass Brothers lent them their $1 million deposit with Cobb personally guaranteeing the secured note. Cobb and team then flew from Fort Worth to New York and arrived in New York about 6 a.m. without so much as a change of clothes. They checked into a hotel, showered, and proudly presented their $300 million-plus offer with the $2 million nonrefundable deposit to the 8 a.m. Penn Central executive committee meeting prior to the 5 p.m. full board meeting.

The executive committee turned down the Cobb/Bass offer because Penn Central's chairman had a handshake agreement with the senior executives of Equitable and felt an obligation to sell to Equitable. Although the chairman was the largest shareholder of Penn Central, Cobb reminded him that he did not have the fiduciary authorization to sell this asset without full board approval and that the Arvida management and the Bass Brothers were prepared to pay more than Equitable Life. The chairman responded that the executive committee had voted unanimously to sell to Equitable and that this would be discussed at the board meeting later that afternoon.

An hour later, the general counsel of Penn Central advised Cobb that he should not come to the board meeting because of his potential conflict of interest. As a Penn Central board member and fiduciary of all the Penn Central shareholders, Cobb responded that he knew the Arvida management/Bass Brothers proposal was superior to the Equitable offer and that his presence in the board meeting was imperative to protect the interest of the Penn Central shareholders by ensuring acceptance of the best proposal. At the 5 p.m. board meeting, Cobb's argument prevailed, and the board agreed to sell to Arvida management and the Bass Brothers but with a higher nonrefundable deposit. Fortunately, the Bass Brothers' analysis of the Arvida financial statements and appraisals confirmed Cobb's enthusiasm, and the transaction concluded a few months later.

DISNEY MERGER

In early 1984, about six months after Arvida management and the Bass Brothers purchased Arvida Corporation, Saul Steinberg (a well-known corporate raider) made a proposal to purchase all of the common stock of the Walt Disney Company and announced that if he succeeded in this purchase, he would split the Walt Disney Company into three components: a motion picture company in which Steinberg would be in partnership with Kirk Kerkorian, a real estate company that would be in partnership with the Fisher brothers of New York, and a theme park company in which Saul Steinberg would be the major shareholder. Disney's top management believed they had the skills to develop the motion picture and theme park portions of the business, but they knew they did not have the skills to develop Disney's extensive and valuable real estate holdings. A merger with Arvida could provide both the real estate development skills Disney needed and the stability of the wealthy Bass family as a major shareholder to challenge Steinberg. Cobb and Rainwater proposed to Disney's board and management that Disney and Arvida merge, making the Arvida shareholders Disney shareholders. After a few weeks of negotiations, Disney agreed to give the Arvida shareholders a significant pre-

mium for their Arvida shares. A merger agreement was signed between Disney and Arvida on May 9, 1984, and closed on June 5, 1984.

As part of the merger agreement, Cobb joined Disney's board of directors, representing the selling shareholders of Arvida, and Cobb agreed to be chairman and CEO of the newly formed Disney Development Company in addition to his role as chairman of Arvida Corporation. Cobb and the Arvida team played a key role in the new development directions at Walt Disney World in Florida, Disneyland in California, and the purchase of 5,000 acres for Euro Disney near Paris, France.

U.S. DEPARTMENT OF COMMERCE AND AMBASSADOR

In 1987 Cobb was active in assisting Vice President George H.W. Bush in his run for the presidency. Future governor of Florida Jeb Bush had been a partner in Arvida's Cocoplum development. Jeb had introduced Cobb to Vice President Bush, and Cobb was convinced that Vice President Bush would be a great president. During their conversation on the campaign trail, the vice president asked Cobb whether he was interested in joining the Reagan/Bush Administration. Cobb enthusiastically expressed his interest and then met with President Reagan and Secretary of Commerce Malcolm Baldrige. He was nominated and then confirmed by the Senate to be assistant secretary of the U.S. Department of Commerce in charge of trade development.

Cobb's role as assistant secretary for trade development put him in charge of about 500 professionals representing every manufacturing and service industry in the United States. A high percentage of these experts had PhDs or other advanced degrees in various technologies. Their mission was to analyze all trade disputes on behalf of U.S. companies. During Cobb's tenure, major trade negotiations included those with Japan regarding trade of semi-conductors and coal, and the construction of Kansai Airport outside of Kyoto, and the debate between Boeing and Airbus regarding illegal subsidies and selling aircraft at prices below cost.

When Baldrige died in a rodeo accident, President Reagan promoted Cobb to be undersecretary of commerce and gave him responsibility for U.S. travel and tourism. These responsibilities—to encourage and promote international tourism—were equivalent to those of the minister of tourism in most countries. Cobb created several cooperative agreements with U.S. airlines, hotels, rental car companies, and with California, Florida, and other states that were aggressively advertising for international tourists. Cobb worked with Congress and the Department of State to create a visa waiver program that enabled countries friendly with the United States to send their citizens to the United States without a visa, enabling a dramatic increase in international tourist visits.

In 1989, after George H.W. Bush was elected president, he asked Cobb to be the ambassador to the Republic of Iceland. Later that year, Cobb was confirmed by the Senate and moved with his wife, Sue, to Reykjavik. Cobb's primary responsibility as ambassador to Iceland was to advance NATO's military interest there. NATO's primary anti-submarine warfare center was in Iceland because of its proximity to the Soviet Union's submarine bases. Before November 1989, the United States and NATO wanted to increase the anti-submarine warfare capacity beyond the 6,000 Americans stationed there and to increase the number of aircraft and aircraft facilities. Within weeks of Cobb's arrival in Reykjavik, the Berlin Wall fell, the Soviet Union collapsed, and Cobb's responsibilities made a 180-degree turn. Now he was charged to lead the U.S. effort in shrinking its military presence in Iceland.

In 1987, at approximately the same time that Cobb joined the Reagan/Bush Administration, Disney decided to sell Arvida to JMB Realty of Chicago. Twenty of Cobb's colleagues in Arvida decided to leave the firm and form Cobb Partners. In addition, Cobb Partners purchased Arvida Disney's mortgage company, which they sold a few years later. Although Cobb was a large shareholder in Cobb Partners, his government responsibilities prevented him from being an officer or director.

COBB PARTNERS AND PAN AM

In 1992, Cobb was asked to be on the board of directors of a new Pan Am that was going to be formed by Delta Airlines out of Pan Am's earlier bankruptcy. Delta would control this new airline, but outside public shareholders would include Cobb and others. In the middle of these negotiations, Delta pulled out and Cobb was left negotiating with the trustees of the Pan Am bankruptcy.

As part of these negotiations, Cobb purchased all of the intellectual property of Pan Am and all of the marketing assets and the 4 million-member Pan Am World Pass program. Cobb announced that rather than form a new airline, he would create a Pan Am alliance of smaller international carriers and focus on a Pan Am marketing company that would manage the World Pass program. Cobb found interest from several Latin American carriers, a dozen or so European and Middle Eastern

carriers, and about an equal number of Asian carriers. All of these carriers stated that the Pan Am alliance needed a U.S. carrier to connect JFK, Miami, and Los Angeles international airports. Cobb was unsuccessful in convincing any U.S. airline to join the Pan Am alliance until Marty Shugrue, the liquidator of Eastern Airlines' assets, showed a great interest. Shugrue, had been the COO of Pan Am and the CEO of Continental and Eastern airlines.

As it turned out, Shugrue could get financing for the new Eastern Airlines only if Cobb agreed to contribute all his Pan Am assets for stock in this new Pan Am/Eastern combination. Cobb reluctantly agreed to this merger and also agreed to be the chairman of the board of this new Pan Am, even though he had not wanted to get into the airline business. This proved to be one of Cobb's few failures. The new Pan Am was not successful in competing with American Airlines and other competitors and eventually filed for bankruptcy a second time.

SKI RESORT COMMUNITIES AND OTHER BOARDS

During the early 1990s, Cobb purchased investments in Telluride, Durango, and Kirkwood resort communities. Other investments followed in the late 1990s and early 2000s.

Through these various relationships, Cobb served on the board of directors of nine publicly traded corporations: Arvida, Penn Central, Walt Disney, LNR Property Corporation, WCI Communities, Ameritas, Pan Am Corporation, CLC of America, and Southeast Banking. He also served on the boards of many privately held corporations.

EDUCATION, INTERNATIONAL, AND CIVIC AFFAIRS

Cobb has been very active with the University of Miami. For the past 35 years, he has served as a trustee, with 20 of those years as the vice chair and chair of the board of trustees. At Barry University in Miami, Cobb started an on-campus charter school for grades 6, 7, and 8. Barry University awarded Cobb an honorary doctorate for founding this school and for other community activities. Cobb is a former trustee of the Stanford University alumni endowment funds. He was also the chairman of the Florida Business/Higher Education Partnership, which was a group of Florida corporate CEOs and university presidents building a coalition for Florida's higher education system.

In the late 1970s, Cobb created the South Florida Coordinating Council, which consisted of the 100 largest companies in south Florida, to address regional issues of transportation, education, and economic development. These regional issues were critical to Arvida's success, as they were to other large South Florida companies. Forcing Dade, Broward, and Palm Beach counties to work together on a regional basis earned Cobb the title "Simón Bolívar of South Florida." Today, thanks to his work, the three south Florida counties do a better job of regionalism and coordinating activities, but in the 1970s regionalism was an alien concept.

For the past 40 years, Cobb has been a member of the Florida Council of 100, an organization of Florida's top 100 business executives assisting Florida's governors. Cobb has been the chairman and a leader of this organization and consequently has been a close confidant of all Florida's governors during the last 40 years, both Democrat and Republican. Reubin Askew, Bob Graham, Bob Martinez, Lawton Chiles, Jeb Bush, Charlie Crist, and Rick Scott have all worked with Cobb on education, economic development, and other issues important to Florida's growth. All of these former governors have concluded that international trade is critical to Florida's economy and have invited Cobb to participate with them on international trade missions. Several large international companies decided to locate their American headquarters operations in the Arvida Park of Commerce or other Arvida projects because of these trade missions. For example, the German company, Siemens, selected the Arvida Park of Commerce after a visit by Governor Askew and Chuck Cobb to Siemens headquarters in Munich.

Cobb has continued his interest in international affairs. Governors Jeb Bush, Charlie Crist, and Rick Scott have asked Cobb to be the chairman of Gateway Florida and Florida FTAA (Free Trade Area of the Americas), the two organizations advancing the state's diplomatic agendas. In addition, Cobb has created and funded a $10,000 annual award that goes to the best U.S. career ambassador in advancing U.S. commercial interests and exports. He is on the boards of the Woodrow Wilson International Center for Scholars, the Dwight D. Eisenhower Fellows Program, the James Madison Institute, the Council on Foreign Relations, the Council of American Ambassadors, and other international organizations. Cobb's deep interest in international issues grew from accompanying Florida's governors to international locations to encourage companies to locate in Florida as part of his work to help develop jobs in Arvida communities.

Cobb has also served as a trustee and board member of his church as well as other civic organizations. He has been a trustee of ULI and governor of the ULI Foundation. Cobb has received many awards, including the Order of the Falcon Grand Cross Star from the nation of Iceland, the National Conference of Christians and Jews Silver Medallion Award, the South Florida Achievement of the Decade Award, the Harvard Business School of South Florida Business Statesman of the Year Award, and the Lifetime Achievement Award from the ULI Southeast Florida/Caribbean District Council.

THE COBB FAMILY

Cobb has been married for 52 years to Sue M. Cobb, who is the former U.S. ambassador to Jamaica, making the Cobb family one of a very few in American history that have had both husband and wife serving as U.S. ambassadors. Sue Cobb was also Florida secretary of state and an attorney who practiced law for many years at the firm of Greenberg Traurig. She was a champion tennis player and skier. In 1988, she attempted to be the first American woman to reach the summit of Mount Everest. Although she did get to 27,000 feet that summer, 100-mile-per-hour winds and other storms prevented her team from reaching the top.

The Cobbs have two sons: Chris, who is an architect, private entrepreneur, and real estate developer, and a graduate of the Harvard Business School, and Toby, who is the co-CEO of LNR Corporation, which manages over $100 billion of commercial real estate securities. He is a graduate of New York University's School of Business. Chris and his wife, Kolleen, have four children; and Toby and his wife, Luisa, have three children, totaling seven grandchildren for Chuck and Sue.